When the Son Frees You

WHEN THE SON FREES YOU

A Catholic Man's Journey of Healing
From Same-Sex Attraction

A. J. Benjamin

Rich ! thanks ! for everything !

TAN Books
Charlotte, North Carolina

Lovingly consecrated to Our Lady of Fatima in anticipation of the Triumph of her Immaculate Heart and placed under the patronage of Pope St. John Paul the Great, who blessed the Church with the gift of the Theology of the Body, and showed me what a "real man" looks like, "Be Not Afraid!"

Bóg Zapłać!

To my dear, patient, and loving wife, without whose support and encouragement I could never have written this book. I love you always!

Jesus then said to the Jews who had believed in him, "If you continue in my word, you are truly my disciples, and you will know the truth, and the truth will make you free." They answered him, "We are descendants of Abraham and have never been slaves to anyone. What do you mean by saying, 'You will be made free'?"

Jesus answered them, "Truly, truly, I tell you, everyone who commits sin is a slave to sin. The slave does not continue in the house forever; the son continues forever. So if the Son makes you free, you will be free indeed. I know that you are descendants of Abraham; yet you seek to kill me, because my word finds no place in you. I speak of what I have seen with my Father, and you do what you have heard from your father." (Jn 8:31–38)

And he who sat upon the throne said, "Behold, I make all things new." Also he said, "Write this, for these words are trustworthy and true." And he said to me, "It is done! I am the Alpha and the Omega, the beginning and the end. To the thirsty I will give water without price from the fountain of the water of life. He who conquers shall have this heritage, and I will be his God and he shall be my son. But as for the cowardly, the faithless, the polluted, as for murderers, fornicators, sorcerers, idolaters, and all liars, their lot shall be in the lake that burns with fire and brimstone, which is the second death." (Rv 21:5–8)

Christ, the final Adam, by the revelation of the mystery of the Father and His love, fully reveals man to man himself and makes his supreme calling clear. *(Second Vatican Ecumenical Council, Gaudium et Spes, no.* 22)

The body, in fact, and only the body, is capable of making visible what is invisible: the spiritual and the divine. It has been created to transfer into the visible reality of the world the mystery hidden from eternity in God, and thus be a sign of it. (Pope St. John Paul II, *Theology of the Body*, February 20, 1980)

Contents

Foreword

Nothing is more powerful than a testimony. The first time a person shared the best news that mankind ever received, it was in the form of a testimony.

Prophets had foretold it, mankind longed for it, but no one could have imagined it would be this good. That GOD would become one of us. I think even the angel Gabriel was stunned at the news he was given to deliver to Mary.

And after receiving Jesus, Mary was propelled by the love within her to reach out to help her cousin Elizabeth who was also pregnant—and her first words to Elizabeth didn't come in the form of a proposition to consider, but an announcement of what God had done in her: "My soul proclaims the greatness of the Lord." Testimony. She wasn't glorifying God "out there," but within her. She was bursting forth with joy about what he had done in her life. And she wanted the world to see that glory shining from inside of her because it was simply too good to keep to herself.

That's what Saints do for us. They help us see the glory of God—shining through them, bursting forth from them. I think that unique way of seeing God's glory will make heaven more beautiful. Saints make heaven more beautiful. The Saints (both capital and lower case) are like crystals that allow the light of God to shine in them, and that light refracts and blasts forth from each in an unrepeatable way—filling the space with their own colors and shapes. But here on earth, that uniquely refracted light has the practical purpose of being easier on the eyes than staring directly at the sun. In other words: It's sometimes easier to grasp the Gospel and how to live it here and now when we see it "enfleshed" in holy lives.

But more. The testimony of saints also makes the Gospel attractive. In the words of Pope Benedict XVI, "The ultimate apologetic (that is, the ultimate answer to people's questions about Faith) is Saints." One can always come up with new objections and questions when you offer them answers. That's because so often those questions come from the will, not the intellect. People come up with questions because they want those questions as excuses to keep them from a way of life they perceive as unattractive. But saints are attractive. They're beautiful. When we see the beaming face of pregnant Mary saying "my soul proclaims the greatness of the Lord!" we don't have questions. We just want some of what she has. All the powers of hell and all the objections of mankind are dumb and silent when they come face to face with a saint.

And when it comes to the most contentious issues of our day, the response of saints offering testimony is the only thing that will work in the end.

We can offer logical responses to attacks on the Church's teaching on homosexuality, sexual ethics, gay marriage, and gender identity, and we should. But as we've seen, those arguments aren't getting us very far.

What we need is a growing "cloud of witnesses" willing to say, "I've been there and done that. I've seen what the world has to offer, and I've found something better—immeasurably better—in Jesus Christ. Fulfillment isn't found in sexual license, but in the love of God. My identity isn't found in my sexual attractions but in him. I am not an L, G, B, or T; I am a child of the most high. My soul proclaims the greatness of the Lord! I have found real love, real peace, real relationships, real joy, real LIFE in him. And it's better than I could have imagined."

People might disagree with our teachings, but like it or not, every human being is attracted to the light of saints sharing their joy.

That's why the book you're holding is so important. Whether you or someone you know has personally struggled with same sex attraction or not, I pray the testimony herein inspires you to deeper faith in the fulfillment of all desire: Jesus Christ.

And I'd ask you to join me in prayer that A. J.'s voice helps inspire a revolution—giving courage to the growing army of people who have experienced same sex attraction or gender confusion and found life, not in the empty propositions of a secular movement, but by following Jesus Christ in his Church.

Chris Stefanick

Preface

"Open Wide the Doors to Christ!"

Do not be afraid. Open wide the doors to Christ! To His saving power open the boundaries of States, economic and political systems, the vast fields of culture, civilization and development. Do not be afraid. Christ knows "what is in man". He alone knows it. So often today man does not know what is within him, in the depths of his mind and heart. So often he is uncertain about the meaning of his life on this earth. He is assailed by doubt, a doubt which turns into despair. We ask you therefore, we beg you with humility and trust, let Christ speak to man. He alone has words of life, yes, of eternal life.[1]

Arguably one of the holiest and most powerful saints in the history of the Church, Pope John Paul "the Great" put forth this charge to the Church in the homily of his inaugural Mass on October 22, 1978. He looked out over a sea of

---

[1] John Paul II, "Homily of His Holiness John Paul II for the Inauguration of His Pontificate," Mass at the Beginning of the Pontificate, October 22, 1978, http://w2.vatican.va/content/john-paul-ii/en/homilies/1978/documents/hf_jp-ii_hom_19781022_inizio-pontificato.html.

humanity with the scarlet specter of communism lurking over them, seeking to devour.

Against it stood this stout and strong Polish pope, who experienced firsthand the oppression of the Nazi and then the communist regimes. Undoubtedly, the pope was referring to the latter in this homily, particularly as he referenced "states" and "economic and political systems." By the grace of Divine Providence, those same systems would fall, not with a bloody war, but with barely a whimper just a little bit more than a decade later.

However, there is something more here that the Holy Spirit inspired the pope to speak about, a greater evil than even communism. It is the secularist idea that life is meaningless, that there really is no God, no absolute truth, and no objective morality to which all are bound regardless of "culture, civilization and development." It was this emptiness that John Paul II would ultimately need to address even after the fall of the Soviet Union and its satellite governments.

Thus, if God is not really in charge, it is left to the state or culture to fill the vacuum and to "save" people from themselves. There is no morality, then, except that which is dictated by the state and culture. People are "free" to do as they wish. Yet ultimately, this Polish pope knew that this "freedom" could and would only end in despair and what he would later refer to as a "culture of death."

The answer to all this? *Be not afraid! Open wide the doors to Christ!*

So, taking up the call of this great saint which he would repeat so many times throughout his glorious pontificate, I now share my story of how Christ transformed me when

I opened wide my doors to him. Truly, as the Second Vatican Council taught, Jesus Christ fully revealed *this* man to himself.

Although this is a book for anyone seeking a closer walk with the Lord, I write especially for men. At this point in our culture, masculinity is often taken for granted and not valued. The truth is that it is masculinity which makes up the power of Christianity. Jesus Christ was incarnate of the Virgin Mary as a *man*.

This is no accident. God could have incarnated as a woman or even a sexless angelic being, but he chose to be born a man. The truth is that men are the spiritual centers of the Church.

Both men and women are made in his divine image, but only men can physically represent him in their own bodies. Men represent God without even trying—our male bodies just do it for us! Thus, we men have great calling to ensure that we present the world as true an image of him as possible.

I learned this the hard way through my own struggles with my own masculinity, particularly in the area of homosexuality, specifically same-sex attraction (SSA). Although most men probably don't have a prolonged struggle with SSA, I think it is fair to say that many men do struggle with masculinity in some way, due largely to our relationships with our fathers or other elder male relatives in our lives. We also struggle because of the poor examples male culture presents in our society. The main goal for the unredeemed man is selfish pleasure, an approach to relationships that looms large in what John Paul II correctly called the "culture of death."

This is not the manhood of Jesus Christ. His true manhood is reflected in what we read in the Gospels. There we see a man of uncompromising strength and power who literally loved unto *death*, with bountiful compassion and mercy. He is a man who models for us an unwillingness to compromise his principles, who is willing to sacrifice for others even to the point of shedding his own blood. This is Jesus Christ.

This is Masculinity Incarnate.

This is the One for whom you have waited all your life.

Fall in love with him.

You won't be disappointed.

I wasn't.

Be not afraid.

Acknowledgments

In such an endeavor as this, there are so many people who contribute in so many ways, both small and great, that it is almost impossible to thank them all. Invariably, I know I have left some folks out, and for that, I apologize!

First, I want to thank Our Lord and Savior Jesus Christ for showering his many blessings upon me. I am truly humbled by the call he has given me to help in the building of his kingdom. It is a rare honor to be able to share my story with a wider audience in the form of this book; it is not an honor and responsibility I take lightly.

One of the greatest gifts Our Lord gave me is his own Blessed Mother as my great patroness. She has truly been my pillar of fire who has guided me throughout my life and never abandoned me, even when I wished she would have. I am *totus tuus, Maria*, and always will be!

Next, this book never would have happened without the love, encouragement, and support of my wife. Her faith and love has supported me not only during this process but throughout our whole marriage. She is not only my wife but my best friend. The Lord has truly blessed me.

Similarly, to be successful in life, I believe a man needs a band of brothers to accompany him on his life journey. I have been blessed with so many of these along the way, both those mentioned within these pages and outside them. They make me the man I am.

I am also deeply grateful for the amazing folks at TAN Books and am edified both by the faith they put in me as a new, inexperienced author and their strength and courage in taking on a book about an issue few are willing to talk about honestly.

Finally, I would like to thank my good friend and brother Chris Stefanick of *Real Life Catholic* for writing this amazing foreword. He is a true giant among men and one of the most authentically holy men I have I ever met. I am honored to stand "back-to-back" with him in this battle for souls.

As far as the actual writing of the book goes, I am greatly indebted to Dr. Michael Hahn for his thorough and exacting critique of the original draft. It was his indispensable guidance and direction that helped me to release the proverbial sculpture from inside its block of rough marble.

I would also like to thank Mike Aquilina, executive vice-president of the Saint Paul Center for Biblical Theology, for his encouragement, mentoring, and advocacy through the publication process. I would not be here today without his help!

In addition, I received so much great feedback during the editing from so many sources. Chief among them are my good friends and brothers Jonathan, Joe, and Bill. Their excellent and exhaustive feedback helped me to "fine tune" and focus my ideas to create something that I hope will edify all and build up Holy Mother Church in this age of great crisis.

Finally, thank *you* for reading!

On My "Coming Out"

I used to be gay. Sort of.

But I don't really consider myself "ex-gay" either.

The "gay" label is a social construct that has no objective basis in true reality. When we don't understand something, we tend to make up all sorts of labels to help fit it into our subjective experience.

The trouble is, at least for me, the label just doesn't fit.

It never really did.

"Ex-gay" doesn't really fit either.

You can't replace one inaccurate term with another.

I'm not now any more "ex-gay" than I was "gay" in the first place.

What I am, however, is a man who has experienced predominant sexual and romantic attraction to other men throughout much of my life from as early as I can remember. Through twenty-plus years of healing and self-discovery, I have seen those attractions diminish to the point where I am very happily married with three children.

Yes, of course to a woman.

Ok. Then I must be "bisexual," right?

Nope.

That's another label that fits me about as well as the previous two.

I'm kind of hard to get a handle on, aren't I?

Guilty as charged.

This stuff is hard to talk about. That's why we need to. That's why I'm "coming out" and writing this book.

You see, I made a promise to Our Lady of Fatima back in 1996 that if she would show me the way to healing my own homosexuality, I would do everything in my power to share this healing with other men who struggle under the weight of this same cross.

The Mother of Jesus is such a good and caring mother.

She did it.

She showed me the way.

So here I am, fulfilling my end of the bargain.

Let me tell you what this book is about and what it is *not* about.

If you are looking for an explosive story about a guy with a bunch of gay lovers, or one who was hopelessly addicted to gay porn or who was a mover and a shaker in the gay lifestyle and then had a conversion, that's not me. There are plenty of those stories out there and some of them are quite compelling and well worth reading.

But that's not me.

Never was.

I've never had sex with a man, and although I've looked at pornographic images of men, masturbated with those images, and entertained a lurid homosexual fantasy life for many years, I thankfully never became addicted. I never really embraced the whole gay rights thing either, and I was always a believing Catholic, even when I really didn't want to be.

Sounds kind of boring, huh?

It's OK. You won't hurt my feelings.

From the outside looking in, it probably is pretty mundane and, yeah, maybe even a little *boring*.

The thing is, once you let the Lord Jesus into your life and allow him to take full control, life is never boring again.

That's the essence of my story. The Lord Jesus Christ and his Blessed Mother saved me from myself and my own darkness.

I wrote this book to show how a personal relationship with Jesus Christ (particularly through the sacraments) and devotion *and total consecration*[2] to the Virgin Mary can give a very ordinary man some *very* extraordinary grace.

Really, if you looked at me, nothing in my life would stand out. I am a happily married father of three wonderful children, and I live in a middle-class suburban town.

Professionally, I am public high school English teacher and a part-time adjunct college professor.

I am a lifelong Catholic Christian who is very active in my parish running a successful men's ministry, among other things.

That's it! There's no big story.

Yet, doesn't the Lord approach us in our ordinariness?

So, if he did it for this not-so-special guy, why couldn't he do it for anyone? Why wouldn't he? Do we not believe in the power of the cross and the Resurrection?

I'm not just talking about men who experience sexual attraction to other men.

I'm talking to everyone because we all have something from which we need to be saved or we would not need a

---

2   See Louis De Montfort, *True Devotion to Mary: With Preparation for Total Consecration* (Charlotte, NC: TAN Books, 2010).

Savior. If you say you don't, then you are either not being honest with yourself or just aren't aware of it.

Maybe you think you're a "good person" who really doesn't do much wrong. Maybe you *are*. But I guarantee that he can make you better and you *do* need his salvation.

We all do.

Even the Virgin Mary, who was herself immaculately conceived and, thus, was created free from all stain of sin and its effects from the first moment of her existence says under the inspiration of the Holy Spirit in Luke 1:46-47, "My soul magnifies the Lord, and my spirit rejoices in God my *Savior!*" (emphasis mine).

Even the Mother of Jesus is *saved*. She needed him too! And she knew it. Her freedom depended on his salvific grace just like everyone else's. What has Jesus Christ saved *you* from? Have you figured that out yet? It's the most important question you will ever have to answer. Maybe my story will help you get to know this *Savior* Jesus or maybe know him better than you do now.

Although my main purpose in writing is to tell my story of how Jesus Christ freed me and to inspire hope in others who struggle similarly, the truth is that we all struggle with something and that anyone can find solace and peace in Christ. In the Gospel, he says, "Come to me, all who labor and are heavy laden, and I will give you rest. Take my yoke upon you, and learn from me; for I am gentle and lowly in heart, and you will find rest for your souls. For my yoke is easy, and my burden is light" (Mt 11:28–30).

Come and make your rest in him!

On Being "Gay" and
Being "Ex-Gay"

Before I go on with my story, let's clarify some terms so you understand what I mean when I say things later on in the book. This is so necessary in today's sex-obsessed world, where nuances can mean a world of difference

Men who identify themselves as "gay" define themselves by their sexual attraction to other men. This becomes the main, if not the *only* definition of themselves in relation to others and the world. Many men who identify this way (even those who are celibate) may sincerely believe that they were "born this way" and that it is an immutable part of who they are.

For a man who self-identifies as gay, any challenge to his same-sex attraction or sexual habits may be viewed as discriminatory and therefore an attack on his person. Most in the gay community usually make no distinction between identity and act.

Thus, if someone offers another viewpoint, it is often met with hostility, and the people who disagree are just labeled as "bigots" and 'haters," which is understandable from that point of view. There may even be some truth to that.

Many people who call themselves Christians do not necessarily have love in their hearts or they may act out of ignorance or fear. Some of them may even have unresolved sexual issues of their own. In any case, prejudice or abuse of anyone, regardless of sexual orientation, is still abuse and is to be soundly condemned as the Church has consistently taught. The *Catechism of the Catholic Church* notes, "The number of men and women who have deep-seated homosexual tendencies is not negligible. This inclination, which is objectively disordered, constitutes for most of them a trial. They must be accepted with respect, compassion, and sensitivity. Every sign of unjust discrimination in their regard should be avoided. These persons are called to fulfill God's will in their lives and, if they are Christians, to unite to the sacrifice of the Lord's Cross the difficulties they may encounter from their condition."[3]

On the opposite side of the spectrum, there is a similar confusion caused by politicians, educators, and medical and mental health "professionals" who erroneously proffer the idea that homosexuality is inborn and only a natural variant of human sexuality. Any attempt to suggest that there may be another "alternative" is quickly attacked by these folks who claim to be "open-minded" and "accepting" of others.

Those who may see things differently are, at best, vilified or, at worst, threatened with loss of livelihood, tax status, the right to speak, and in some cases, violence or imprisonment. Christians should not be surprised then when we are viewed

---

[3]   *Catechism of the Catholic Church,* 2nd. ed. (Washington, DC: United States Catholic Conference, 2000), 2358.

as "bigots" if we challenge what has become in our society—and I do not choose these words lightly—a *golden calf.*

Once the golden calf is erected (see Ex 32), this idol takes the place of the true Divinity. The "gay community" centers not around Jesus but around being gay. Even communities who call themselves Christian *and* gay tend to be less focused on Jesus Christ and more on affirming their own gay identity.

The Lord Jesus rightly pointed out that man cannot serve two masters (see Mt 6:24) because he would grow to love one and hate the other. Jesus Christ must always be the center of our identity because he and he alone "fully reveals man to himself."[4]

Anything else is an idolatrous counterfeit.

Regardless of our sins and shortcomings, the questions you and I need to ask ourselves are the following: Is Jesus Christ the center of my identity? Is his will the sole criterion by which I live my life? Am I willing to get rid of anything, *anything* in my life that is not his will?

If we cannot honestly answer yes to any of those questions, then we are guilty of idolatry.

The archbishop of Philadelphia, Charles Chaput, put it best when he said the following on October 20, 2014 after a speech at the *First Things* Erasmus Lecture, in New York City, "We have deep respect for people with same-sex attraction, but we can't pretend that they're welcome on their own terms. None of us are welcome on our own terms in the

---

[4]   *Gaudium et Spes,* 22, http://www.vatican.va/archive/hist_councils/ ii_vatican_council/documents/vat-ii_cons_19651207_gaudium- et-spes_en.html.

Church; we're welcome on Jesus' terms. That's what it means to be a Christian—you submit yourself to Jesus and his teaching, you don't recreate your own body of spirituality."[5] That being said, consider these questions carefully. *Can* a man actually change his sexual orientation? Should he? Does God or the Catholic Church require that he do so?

These are really great questions and ones that are very controversial even among those of us who have struggled with same-sex attraction (SSA) yet are committed to living a chaste life in accordance with the Church's teachings.

According to the *Catechism*, the only thing that is required of people with same-sex attraction is that they remain chaste according to their state in life. "Homosexual persons are called to chastity. By the virtues of self-mastery that teach them inner freedom, at times by the support of disinterested friendship, by prayer and sacramental grace, they can and should gradually and resolutely approach Christian perfection."[6] No one is under any moral obligation to try to undergo sexual orientation change efforts, more commonly known as SOCE, or as some erroneously call it, "conversion" therapy.

People on both sides of the question of orientation change have deeply held views. On the one hand, there are those who believe that the gay identity is a part of who they are and that as long as they are chaste, struggle against sin, and have Jesus Christ in the center of their lives, that is all they

---

5   Charles J. Chaput, "Strangers in a Strange Land," *First Things*, January 1, 2015, https://www.firstthings.com/article/2015/01/ strangers-in-a-strange-land.

6   *Catechism of the Catholic Church*, no. 2359.

need. Many of these folks are quite content with their lives and have no desire to change or may have tried it and not gotten the results they wanted. This might work for some people as long as their identity in Christ is primary.

However, there are also those of us who have experienced a minimization or elimination of same-sex attraction in our lives. Men like me believe that adopting a gay identity is not at the fundamental core of our being and is generally not helpful. We know that our sexual orientation cannot be *cured* as if it were an illness, but we also know that it is much more fluid and that *at least some change* is possible *for at least some people.*

Before I started on my journey of healing, my viewpoint used to be more that of the former group than the latter. I thought that I had to accept my same-sex attraction as immutable and be celibate for the rest of my life.

At one point during my teenage years, I remember seeing the evangelist Pat Robertson's show, the *700 Club.* Although not a regular viewer, I happened to have had it turned on one day when the topic concerned "changing" one's sexual orientation. There were alleged "straight" men on the show who had "changed" from "being gay."

It was my first introduction to "ex-gay" ministries. While I am convinced that true conversions of heart occurred in the lives of some of these men, *ex-gay* is a term that turns many away from these ministries and is, in a certain sense, a misnomer. That language does not exactly match everyone's experience and can come across as offensive to those folks who choose not to pursue SOCE, so I try to avoid that term when describing myself.

The term implies that there is somehow a change in the essence of the person. In reality, who I am never changed, but God led me through a series of conversions that led to a new, wonderful, and deeper understanding of myself.

It's the same problem with calling SOCE "conversion" therapy. "Reparative" therapy is much more accurate.

In a sense, I agree with those who say they are "changed" in that I, too, experienced deep healing and a diminishment of attraction to and desire for sex with men.

But I am still me. I'm just a better, more integrated, more healed me. I wouldn't say that I am "ex" anything. I'm still the same guy I always was.

In any case, though, when I first saw that show, I actually laughed. Did those naïve Protestants really think they could change their orientation simply by "praying away the gay" and hanging out with other men? The idea was ludicrous to me.

As a psychology major in a state university, I had consistently been taught the official American Psychological Association (APA) line that there was nothing wrong with this type of orientation and that it couldn't and *shouldn't* be changed. Anyone who set out to change, my professors and APA orthodoxy said, was simply embarking on an unhealthy path of "internalized homophobia" that would inevitably lead to damage and pain.

I more or less went along with this. While I knew same-sex genital acts were wrong, I also did not believe that Jesus Christ could really change what seemed like such an essential part of who I was.

This is the essential Gospel message I had somehow missed throughout my twenty years as a Catholic and missed again during Pat Robertson's show that day.

Thankfully, I eventually got that message.

However, many don't get it because they follow the lead of the APA and other organizations who say that sexual orientation cannot and should not be changed.

The APA is actually very ambiguous about it. The organization actually backed off an earlier statement which was much stronger, but even from this new and still very biased anti-change view of homosexuality, the one thing that is clear is that nothing is clear.

Here is the revised APA statement of 2008 which can be found on their official website. "There is no consensus among scientists about the exact reasons that an individual develops a heterosexual, bisexual, gay or lesbian orientation. Although much research has examined the possible genetic, hormonal, developmental, social, and cultural influences on sexual orientation, *no findings have emerged that permit scientists to conclude that sexual orientation is determined by any particular factor or factors*. Many think that nature and nurture both play complex roles."[7]

Current research on the origins of homosexuality is even more unclear. In just one example, a 2016 report which claims to give an "up-to-date" summary of modern research

---

[7] *American Psychological Association,* "What causes a person to have a particular sexual orientation?" Answers to your questions: For a better understanding of sexual orientation and homosexuality, last modified 2008, https://www.apa.org/topics/lgbt/orientation, emphasis added.

on the topic pointed out a profound lack of clarity and consistency within the research.[8]

Homosexuality is not an either/or thing. There is no gay gene. That much is conclusive.

So as far as I'm concerned, accepting what the APA has to say about SSA requires a great amount of faith in clearly biased researchers (many of whom are openly gay activists or gay rights sympathizers) who ignore or even attempt to suppress the experience of people like me and many others because we don't fit into their worldview.

Most men who struggle with SSA have stories which are so similar that at times it is uncanny. When we share our stories, we can almost finish each other's sentences. The commonalities are blatantly obvious to us.

So, that being said, does SSA disappear or just become more manageable?

That depends on who you ask. Everyone's experience is different.

Although I still experience attraction to men at times, it really is just a symptom of my own insecurity. I don't know that it will ever go away completely, but honestly, I don't need it to. Everyone struggles with something, and SSA has led me to some of the most incredible relationships I ever thought I'd have and has kept me close to Jesus Christ and the Church. Over and over I hear how my SSA has blessed

8   Lawrence S. Mayer and Paul R. McHugh, "Sexuality and Gender: Findings from the Biological, Psychological and Social Sciences," *The New Atlantis: A Journal of Technology & Society*, no. 50 (Fall 2016): 7-12, https://www.thenewatlantis.com/docLib/20160819_TNA50SexualityandGender.pdf.

my non-SSA friends and how much they value me as a man. I don't think I could ask for more.

That is why I'm telling my story. Whether or not anyone decides to pursue orientation change is a personal decision. We are under no moral obligation to do so. But if anyone chooses not to, I would rather they make an informed choice and talk to people who have actually gone through it. We are out there, and most of us are willing to share.

Don't decide not to because other people (who, quite frankly, ought to know better) say you shouldn't.

Never for one moment did I regret the day I chose to embark on this healing journey, despite the fact that it was very long and, at times, painful. I had to look very deeply at all the dark parts of myself and embrace them, even when I wished, at times, that they weren't there.

Honestly, I think that telling anyone that they can't change or control their unwanted and unhealthy thoughts and desires is untrue, hurtful, irresponsible, and unethical. Imagine if the APA and other "experts" said it about any other condition.

> *"You can't change your addiction to drugs; you just have to accept who you are."*

> *"You can't change your eating disorder; you just have to accept who you are."*

> *"You can't change your depression; you just have to accept who you are."*

> *"You can't change your cutting; you just have to accept who you are."*

Get my point? People would be (rightfully) up in arms, yet somehow it's OK for them to say that seeking to change SSA is "unhealthy" or "dangerous." Many states have even passed laws making it illegal! Why? This is a classic example of the blind leading the blind.

This is such an important issue to me because I was literally ready to kill myself when I believed these lies and distortions. I thank God he swept in when he did and that I heard his voice.

Nowadays, we hear a lot in the media about people killing themselves because they are gay. Usually, though, the media reports that it is because they or those around them couldn't accept that they were gay.

In fact, with the proliferation of pro-gay and pro-gay marriage laws proliferating around the country, we would naturally expect a rise in the mental health of gay men, right? Since the prevailing theory is that the cause of the statistically higher incidents of mental illness in men who identify as gay is institutionalized "homophobia," now that it is rapidly becoming deinstitutionalized by law in most countries of the world, we should naturally see a corresponding rise in mental health among gay men.

However, much to the researchers' surprise, that rise has not happened, and some studies are now noting that the crisis may even be worsening.[9] Researchers note similar trou-

---

9   Sanjay Aggarwal and Rene Gerrets, "Exploring a Dutch paradox: an ethnographic investigation of gay men's mental health," *Culture, Health & Sexuality*, no. 16:2 (2014): 105, https://www.tandfonline.com/doi/abs/10.1080/13691058.2013.841290?journalCode=tchs20.

bling results for "transgender" men and women who have partially or completely "transitioned" to the other sex.[10]

From my perspective, the problem does not seem to be one of homophobia but, rather, the lack of support for men with SSA and a lack of hope.

I wonder how many killed themselves simply because they had no hope because they thought they *had* to be gay?

I could have been one of them.

And I know that there are thousands out there like me.

No matter what the "experts" say or how many laws they pass, I will never stop sharing my story.

If I can give hope to just one man like me, it's worth it.

---

[10]   Lawrence S. Mayer and Paul R. McHugh, 86–108.

Are We Really "Born This Way"?

OK. So now I bet you're thinking, "Well, if men aren't born gay, how do they get that way?"

That's another great question.

First, I want to make a distinction between male and female homosexuality. It is not exactly the same thing either in how it develops in each sex nor in how it manifests itself. I will focus exclusively on the male version since it is the one with which I am most familiar (obviously).

So aren't people who identify as gay "born this way," as the popular notion (and song) goes? Generally speaking, I don't think so. The following Scripture passage is an important one because it explicitly asserts that change is possible. "Do you not know that the unrighteous will not inherit the kingdom of God? Do not be deceived; neither the immoral, nor idolaters, nor adulterers, nor homosexuals, nor thieves, nor the greedy, nor drunkards, nor revilers, nor robbers will inherit the kingdom of God. And such were some of you. But you were washed, you were sanctified, you were justified in the name of the Lord Jesus Christ and in the Spirit of our God" (1 Cor 6:9–11). The reading lists many of the sins which were committed by members of the Corinthian church before being converted to Jesus Christ.

Note that after the list, Saint Paul says, "And such *were* some of you" (emphasis mine). He doesn't say, "And such some of you used to *do*."

So, in other words, at least *some* of the Corinthian Christians left the "gay lifestyle" of their day in order to follow Jesus Christ. There was some sort of an interior change beyond that of just actions. They were then sanctified in his name and presumably left their sinful lives behind. Note also the sins which are held equivalent to homosexual acts: greediness, stealing, gossiping, and drunkenness, among others. Paul's point is that sin is sin and we should not attempt to fool ourselves by saying that what we do is "not *that* bad" compared to someone else.

So, in order to continue the process of perfection in the Christian life during my healing journey, I had to root out the areas of my life where I experienced the proclivity to sin. I knew that one of the first things I had to do was discover the origins of my homosexuality. In the research that I did, which was, admittedly, not approved by today's "psychological experts," it seems that there were some emerging patterns.

Although most therapists and theorists who argue against homosexuality as an "alternative lifestyle" are generally silenced by political and professional peer pressure and even legal maneuvers, there is still a modest body of literature which supports the idea that it is a deviation from normal male sexuality, which is evident from a simple internet search on the topic.

The general theory is that when boys are little, they are at first bonded to their mother during infancy and early childhood. Later, as they grow (around the age of two or three), they begin to separate from their mothers and begin to be attracted to the world of men.

During that time, the healthy boy will detach from the mother and begin bonding with the father and/or other males. If this does not happen (or happens in a way in which the boy cannot relate), the boy will usually find that he has trouble forming a strong masculine identity. Once puberty hits and the sex hormones start kicking in, the sexual drive is then attached to this identity confusion and the struggle becomes sexualized or eroticized in unhealthy ways.

I can understand why people think they are "born gay" though. There may be some genetic predispositions and even some hormone imbalances which could influence a boy to have strong same-sex attractions, but I would question the science behind any experiment which claims to find a "gay" gene, simply because sexual expression is far too varied to be the result of any one genetic switch.[11]

The long and short of it is that if boys who require a lot of male affirmation and love do not get that the way that they need it, they may experience a developmental block, of sorts, which causes their need to become sexualized.

In most of these cases, the feeling of being "different" is probably there for as long as the child can remember, so it

---

[11]   Although a comprehensive treatment of all available literature is beyond the scope pf this book, interested readers should see Joseph Nicolosi, *Reparative Therapy of Male Homosexuality: A New Clinical Approach* (Lanham, MD: Rowman & Littlefield Publishers, 2004), particularly chapters 4–10 and Gerard J. M. Van Den Aardweg, *The Battle for Normality: A Guide for (Self-) Therapy for Homosexuality* (San Francisco, CA: Ignatius Press), chapters 1–4.

should not be surprising to hear men who identify as "gay" say that they have "always" known they were different. I used to feel that way myself. Many gay activists offer this as "proof" that they were "made this way" or even that God desires that they have sex with men.

I can't condemn anyone for the life they lead, because I don't know their personal journey that got them there. I can only say, based on my own experience, that God wanted more for me. I can say, however, that I don't believe that just because a man has same-sex attractions he needs to engage in intercourse with other men, nor do I believe that sex with other men will lead to true joy, peace, and happiness.

Thus, the development of same-sex attraction in men is a complex one that is not easily pigeon-holed. In some of the research I've read, theorists suggest that it is more accurate to refer to it not as homosexuality but rather *homosexualities*. Although I am not trying to make a comparison to a disease model here, we often say that we have a "cold" which delineates a certain set of symptoms which are, in reality, caused by any one of a number of bacteria or viruses. In the same way, same-sex attraction can come about in a large variety of ways, and although there are similarities, no two men have traveled exactly the same path and experience it exactly the same way.

There are, however, a number of commonalities that seem to be present in a lot of these cases. I have attempted to compile a non-exhaustive list of some common factors:

1. Sexual abuse or molestation
2. Physical abuse (by men)

3. Lack of a father figure or other significant male role
    model; sometimes coupled with an overly emotional
    bond with the mother
4. Poor relationships with and/or bullying by male
    peers
5. Body image issues
6. Weak masculine identity
7. Poor boundaries with the mother or mother figure
8. Lack of "investment" in male culture
9. Sexual experimentation with other men or boys,
    often accompanied by use of pornography

Again, this is a somewhat simplistic list about a very complicated and sensitive topic.[12]

Not all factors are present in all situations, and there may
be other factors not on this list, but some combination of
the above factors seems to elevate the risk of same-sex attraction in men, according to the research. One of the fascinating things about humanity is that we truly are, as St. John
Paul II and other personalist philosophers note, unique and
unrepeatable entities. So two different people can experience
similar things and turn out completely different.

For example, how many times have we heard of cases
where people undergo similar horrific abuse and one turns
out to be a serial killer and the other ends up becoming
(sometimes literally) a saint? It is no different with the development of homosexuality. Although I ended up struggling
with same-sex attractions, I know a number of men who

---

[12]   Joseph Nicolosi, *Reparative Therapy of Male Homosexuality: A New
       Clinical Approach.*

had similar life experiences to mine yet do not struggle with homosexuality.

In any case, it really needs to be a "perfect storm" for homosexuality to develop in a man. If some of the factors are not present, it is likely that same-sex attraction won't be present either.[13] For me, most of the factors were, unfortunately, present.

When I first began to look at myself and how I experienced homosexuality, I found that I, more or less, "fit the mold" with one exception. To the best that I can recall, I was never sexually abused or molested. At one point, I almost wished I had been just because then it would have explained why my feelings were so strong and why I desired sex with men so deeply.

I asked a lot of people, both priests and laity, to help me discern whether there was anything in my past that might have led to this. They concurred with me that they also did not discern any spiritual signs of sexual abuse, and one priest even suggested that its absence may have been one of the reasons that I never acted out on my feelings as an adult.

With the issue of sexual abuse out of the way, I was still left with the question of why I had these desires and feelings. As I began my reflections, I did begin to see other patterns in my life which created that "perfect storm." For me there was one single factor that shaped my life and was at the heart of all my struggles: my relationship with my father.

---

[13]   Ibid.

The "Sins of the Father"

Joseph Sciambra is a former homosexual who left that lifestyle and founded an apostolate which ministers to homosexual men. Famous for his T-shirts that correctly but provocatively proclaim that "Jesus Loves Gay Men," he maintains a website and has written a book detailing the dark, occult side of the gay world.

Sciambra lays out his story in all its graphic details in order that people see the life he led for what it was and for the destructive places it led him. Of course, not all men who identify as gay travel the same dark road as Sciambra, but he certainly provides much food for thought and discussion about the spirituality at the core of gay culture. Now a staunch Catholic who has accumulated the wisdom of years, I was struck by a comment he once made on an online forum.

He warned, "Fathers love your sons – or some other man will."

Wow. That's something to meditate on. Even if all of us might not go to the extreme ends of the gay subculture the way Sciambra did, he makes a great point about a father's duty to his children and the disastrous consequences that occur should a father abdicate or abuse that duty.

The truth behind it is that we, as fathers, hold tremendous power over our children. In today's day and age, we men often sort of excuse ourselves from our God-given roles as husbands and underestimate the power of our own masculinity, especially with our children.

Sciambra's observation is one that should resonate with all of us. My lack of connection with my own father was the one core issue that I believe was at the root of all my other issues with men.

I come from a good family. I mean, by today's standards, a *really good*, intact family but by no means a perfect one. Don't get me wrong, like every other family, we had and have our issues, some of them pretty big, but in the end, we stick together. Although we are not always in agreement and we have our share of rough spots along the way, we are still together.

It almost seems as if speaking of some of the dysfunctional aspects of an otherwise functional family is somehow disloyal. Maybe it is, but it's the truth, and the truth, as I found again and again, *always* makes me free.

It took a lot of prayer and healing for me to realize that we are all on the journey and that "all have sinned and fall short of the glory of God" (Rom 3:23).

My family and I are a bunch of sinners, but I also know that beyond a shadow of a doubt, if any of them truly knew how deeply their actions were affecting me at the time, they would have moved heaven and earth to make it right. A part of me wishes I had shared these things then in order to give them that chance.

There were (and are) good reasons not to do so, but not doing so led me down a very lonely road. So this is an analysis, as best I know, of how my own particular struggle developed and how family dynamics, particularly my relationship with my dad, played a part.

As previously mentioned, the key to a healthy sense of the masculine begins with the father-son relationship, then extends to other adult male relationships and then to same-sex peers. A rupture in any of those areas could lead to a distorted sense of masculinity and then possibly homosexuality.

This was especially true of my relationship with my father. From the time I was a child (less than five years of age), we didn't have much in common. There is no such thing as a perfect father, and there is also no such thing as a perfect son. In our father-son relationship, we both sinned.

These are just my perceptions of and reflections on our relationship and the mistakes he made as well as the ones I made and how the interaction of the two resulted in my distorted view of myself.

Looking back on my relationship with my father and the other men in my life, I think it's actually very similar to the relationship many people have with God. A lot of people know a lot about God, but it really doesn't matter how much you know *about* him. It is really about whether you *know* him and are a part of his inner life.

This was the part of manhood from which I felt excluded through my father. Material provision was not the problem. Dad was a not a *good* provider, but a *great* one. I had almost everything a boy could ever want, but I still felt shut out of the inner sanctuary of men. It was not entirely his fault, but the father is the gateway to the male world, and without that connection, it is very difficult for a boy to navigate it. He needs his dad to be his ambassador, as it were, into a strange and foreign land. He needs his dad to tell him how it works and show him the way not only to survive but to *thrive* there.

So back in the beginning when I was younger, my emotional relationship with my father was distant at best. I always felt that I was not the son he wanted or what a boy should be.

He always praised my intelligence and my accomplishments and was always physically present, but I don't think I am the type of son he would have preferred, had he the choice. Quite frankly, I know that I was not the son I would prefer either (at least not then). I can totally see where my sensitive nature would have been very difficult for any father to deal with. My feelings got hurt very easily then and I know I cried a lot, probably over sometimes minor things.

Likewise, Dad seemed pretty indifferent to my sexual identity while I was growing up, but to his credit, he never belittled me when I chose to do activities that were not stereotypically masculine, like sewing, painting, or cooking.

From an early age, I was always called precocious. I started talking in full sentences by the time I was one but didn't begin walking until I was well past two. Anyone who has studied the interactions of males can tell you that this is not a great combination. Most men do not relate verbally but, rather, through activities. See the problem already?

A normal avenue in the development of our relationship was just not there.

It had to be especially hard for Dad the big sports-hero to relate to this sensitive, bookish, intellectual, independent kid with poor sense of hand-eye coordination and a hearing problem. I think we spoke two different languages then. Dad may have felt intimidated by my verbal abilities, so I think he preferred to just let me do as I pleased and not to get too involved with my activities. He probably figured that I didn't really need him, but the truth is that I did.

Even though Dad and I might not have connected in the stereotypical male ways, I think this could have been somehow fixed through other means. What damaged our relationship irreparably was that my father physically abused me.

My dad was a hot-headed, hot-tempered, moody man. I think in my early childhood, he thought that spankings were the best way to accomplish this "quick and easy" punishment. For some boys, when done correctly, this actually might work. The problem was that Dad had a violent and unpredictable temper.

It went beyond the spanking to the point where it was definitely physical abuse, by anyone's definition. I could recount a lot of times when he beat me far beyond what was acceptable. He never hit me with more than his open hand, but when he did, he hit me so hard that I remember the white finger-shaped welts his hands left my skin after he did it and the bruises that did not fade for days.

Instead of simply correcting me, he would vent his own anger and frustration on me. He would hit me repeatedly in my arms, legs, or buttocks as he gave vent to his rage. There were so many of these situations throughout the years and only the circumstances varied. It was the same abusive pattern.

On one particular occasion when I could not have been more than nine or ten, I wanted a dog very badly and was saving money to buy one. Dad had agreed that I could do household chores in order to help earn what I needed. On one particular day, he gave me my wages which I did not think was commensurate with the amount of work I did.

Sensitive child that I was, I cried in my disappointment. Dad's reaction was to knock me to the floor and beat both my arms with both of his hands while yelling at me for being ungrateful. I just remember being so scared and in such pain as I begged him to stop. I don't know how long it actually went on. I just remember being sore for a couple of days afterwards.

On another occasion, I remember him quizzing me on my multiplication tables. I'm not exactly sure what happened next. I don't even remember what I did. I just remember that I was confused about something and questioned him about it. He somehow interpreted this as my being a wise guy and, out of nowhere, slapped my leg in punishment, hard. When I asked him, through tears, what I did wrong and it was clear that I didn't do what he thought I did, he apologized.

But it was too late. The damage was done and my trust in him was broken. Repeatedly.

These are just some stories among many that I could relate, but I think you get the point. In classic abuser pattern, he always said he was sorry after it happened, and I know that he was, but an unpredictably violent father was not a good thing for a sensitive boy who had a weak masculine identity as it was.

During my childhood and early adolescent years, I walked on the proverbial eggshells. Dad was a man of overreaction. Simple things would often set him off, seemingly out of nowhere. When he would have one of his temper outbursts, I would hate to see the whole house in the turmoil he usually put it in, even if he was not violent toward me. There was a true atmosphere of fear and tension.

However, during these times of strife, I felt like I was caught in the middle and was somehow responsible for putting the pieces back together again afterwards. It was a feeling of great helplessness and powerlessness on my part because he was so much bigger and stronger than I was.

Before adolescence, displays of affection between us were few and far between with no more close contact than that of an occasional (and awkward) hug. If the truth be told, I really didn't want any kind of intimacy with him at all. This chasm between Dad and me widened as I grew in age.

It was during the turbulent adolescent years that rather than walk on eggshells around him, I picked up the eggs and threw them at him. I deliberately provoked him. Although he was still bigger than me, I began to rebel against him. I didn't care what he did to me physically.

So whenever he would have an explosion of temper, I matched it as best I could. Looking back, I realize that these were obviously not productive outbursts but, rather, my insecure way of defending myself and, in a certain sense, fighting back. It was the beginning of the anger of a homosexual man.

During these times, I truly hated him and felt nothing but contempt for him and, through him, all men. I vowed that I would *never* be like him when I grew up. Little did I know how powerful my thoughts were and what devastating consequences they would have. Feeding on my own anger towards him did not help my situation.

Primarily through my relationship with Dad, and later ones with other men and boys in my life, I gradually learned that men cause others pain and men are something to be feared.

So much power and so much destruction.

How could a little boy possibly compete?

This was masculinity?

This was manhood?

This was what being a man was all about?

No thanks. I wanted no part of it.

Can you blame me?

So I emotionally distanced myself from my father and shut the door to the world of men. Added to that was that I much preferred the world of Mom to that of Dad. I can remember that I liked it when Dad worked and hated it when he was home. I dreaded having him in the house, and the more he worked, the happier I was.

Conversely, I had a close relationship with my mother all throughout my life. It was she who gave me the affirmation and encouragement that I needed. We did a lot together, and if I had the choice of which parent to do things with, I went with her rather than Dad.

The downside to this was that she thought of me as "her little boy" and we shared a lot of emotionally intimate moments, which quite honestly might have been better shared between her and my father. I think she unconsciously saw me as a confidante who understood her and gave her emotional support that she needed and wasn't getting from my dad.

Ironically, it was she who was more forceful in telling me to "be a man" and avoid stereotypically feminine things, which was really my father's role. She always made sure my clothes and toys were sufficiently masculine. Looking back now, it's easy to see how I had such a tremendous role confusion.

Through his violence, Dad destroyed the father-son relationship between us. Quite honestly, although we later became closer and I grew in respect for him as we both got older and after I had children of my own, and although, before he died, we parted in peace and mutual forgiveness, the wound never completely healed. That is a task for another world.

The truth is, I didn't feel his love when I needed it.

All needed not have been lost, though. Lots of men grew up with abusive fathers and didn't become homosexual.

Boys in such situations at home can sometimes substitute what might be lacking in the relationship with their fathers through relationships with other men in the family or among the social network. I wasn't blessed here either. There were very few men in my family and I never felt especially attached to any of them while growing up.

My only uncle took great care of his family and is lovingly remembered by my aunt and my cousins, but to me, he was a mystery. He died suddenly while he was in his fifties, and I still can't tell you a thing about him except that he golfed and liked to have a good time. They say he was a good man and I never had reason to doubt it, but I couldn't tell you what made him so. While I was growing up, besides my father, he was the only other man on Dad's side of the family.

My mother's side had two men as well, her stepfather and her uncle. Her stepfather, whom we treated like a grandfather, was an alcoholic. I didn't know this growing up and he never mistreated me in any way, but it explained a lot of things after I learned it.

My mother's uncle was a venerable and kind old man. Again, I didn't really know either of them well, primarily because there was a language barrier. They both spoke really harsh, broken English with a heavy accent. Since I am hearing-impaired, it made understanding what they were saying nearly impossible, even though both men seemed to delight in having me around. I never felt "unwanted" by them; I just never felt connected.

This breach with the masculine colored my world in ways that I could not have fathomed back then. It would take me nearly twenty years to fully come to terms with it and another seven to become healed enough that I could function as a heterosexual man. To most outside observers, however, my life must have looked pretty good.

But the truth is, I was a *lost* boy.

So what did I do?

I did what most homosexual men do. I looked for other men to love me, of course.

Fortunately, after a long search, eventually I found them.

And they really loved me and still love me and helped begin to heal that wound.

Not Like the Other Boys

My story begins without fanfare in the turbulence of the mid-seventies. Jimmy Carter was president and St. Paul VI was the pope. Bell-bottoms were in; Vietnam was finally out. Back then *Star Wars* was one low-budget movie that you could only see in the theaters or on cable. We didn't have a VHS or Beta player yet (if you don't know what those are, ask somebody who's forty or older). The radical sixties and seventies had begun to stabilize as the country began to shake itself awake from its drug-induced stupor and move into the relatively conservative Reagan era.

I was a precocious little tyke, they say; I spoke full sentences at eighteen months, and many friends and family joke that I haven't stopped talking yet. I was an imaginative child, and I can specifically remember the genuine amazement of my parents at some of the ideas I would come up with even at an early age.

My childhood was formed in the waning years of the Cold War. We would be fine, though, as long as we could keep "the Russians" and their cronies in check. Again, the more things change, the more they stay the same. With the rest of the world, I rejoiced when the Berlin Wall finally fell and all the communist regimes with it.

We had won . . . or so *we* thought.

Little did we know that it was too late, as Our Lady had warned in Fatima months before the Bolshevik revolution way back in 1917, "If Russia is not converted, then she will spread her errors throughout the world."[14]

Of course, as a child, I barely knew who Our Lady of Fatima was, nor the decisive role she would play in my life many years later. I had many years to live and many lessons to learn before I was ready to have a personal encounter with the Mother of Jesus.

Until that time would come, I entertained myself with the gift of imagination for much of my childhood. There were many periods of loneliness even at a young age; I had very few childhood playmates outside of preschool.

Both my parents worked, and so most of my childhood days (when I wasn't in "nursery school," as they called it then) were spent in the care of my grandparents in Trenton, New Jersey's old Slovak neighborhood. My grandfather's family hailed from Czechoslovakia, and my grandmother's family was Polish. My grandparents were first generation Americans but still held on to their "Old Country" values. Grandmom always referred to their union as a "mixed marriage," which I thought was hilarious since both of them were white and Catholic and from the same general area of the world.

She said their announcement of nuptials raised not a few eyebrows back in the early 1900s, but as she nonchalantly recalled, "People eventually got over it."

---

[14] World Apostolate of Fatima, USA, "July 13, 1917: The Vision of Hell," The Story of Fatima, https://www.bluearmy.com/the-story-of-fatima.

I credit my grandmother with sowing the seeds of faith in me. Despite her sixth-grade education and sometimes abrasive ways, she proved herself a wise and caring woman with a great faith in Jesus Christ in the sacraments and a strong devotion to Our Lady. She was always praying the Rosary or the Saint Ann Novena. She is the one who introduced me to the Stations of the Cross during Lent. She died a holy death complete with Viaticum, the Apostolic Pardon, and visions of angels and "the Lady" coming to escort her home.

My grandfather, on the other hand, who was physically abused by his alcoholic father, seemed very distant to me. He very rarely interacted with me, yet he was always physically present, especially if I needed him. I knew he loved me, but even after he died in 1996, I found that I didn't really know much about him, even though I'd known him all my life. I mean, we have the family stories and we joke about the little quirks of his behavior. We even (half) jokingly refer to him as the "Archie Bunker" of the family (complete with "his chair" and all). I could tell you that I knew *about* Grandpop, but never that I really *knew* Grandpop.

What made him tick?

What were his joys?

What were his struggles?

I will never know.

As a child, my parents would pick me up each day from my grandparents' house and bring me back to the apartment I shared with them in the suburbs. A few weeks before the birth of my sister, when I was five, we moved into a two-story colonial in an "established" neighborhood across town.

While the huge backyard and pool provided more food for my imagination, the older neighborhood did not provide many friends. I went to a Catholic school in the city, so with both my parents working, there was little opportunity for social interaction outside school.

Hanging out with boys my own age just didn't happen. There was no one in my neighborhood with whom I went to school. I basically just played with the few girls my age who lived down the street or my dog (which I did eventually get). When I wasn't doing that, I was watching television or reading books, not socializing myself to the male world.

Indeed, my greatest friend became the television. Once I began to outgrow the drone of television, a new idol replaced it—books. I loved to read. I would devour books one right after the other in what, in retrospect, was a way to avoid a pain and loneliness I didn't even know I was feeling inside.

Looking back, I was probably depressed. One of the reasons I think so is because I was a bed-wetter (which some pediatricians think may be a symptom) until a very late age; I still had fears and occasional instances of it happening as late as fifth grade! There certainly could have been other reasons for the bed-wetting behavior, but I think it is interesting to note that my own son, who is physically a "mini-me," *never* had a problem with it.

Despite the fact that I always had a nagging feeling that I wasn't like other kids, I started off okay. In school, especially in early childhood, I can remember many boys and girls seeking my leadership. For some reason, they always looked to me to make a decision when one needed to be made and would frequently flock around me.

I don't know why, but I remember that I found it really annoying and aggravating that they would hang all over me. The relative "influence" lasted probably until about fifth grade when I became "out of the loop" of the school culture, probably because of location (we lived in a different town from where the school was) and perhaps because of my dormant but slowly emerging homosexuality.

Of course, this was also the time when puberty hit and most kids feel so bad about themselves that they do their utmost to make sure other kids feel as bad as they do. By the time the sixth grade rolled around, I did not feel admired anymore and began to even feel scorned.

I began to be ridiculed on what seemed like a daily basis. What little of my masculine self remained was slowly but surely being eroded by male peers. I suffered so much at the hands of these boys, yet at the same time, I still sought their approval by, in turn, being mean to others boys in a classic example of the victim identifying with his abuser. I did and said a lot of terrible things then which I really regret now.

Where I was not successful with people my own age, I found that I could relate to adults exceedingly well. In fact, I found that I could impress them to no end. I was a favorite among teachers and other adults, but with my peers, my social skills left much to be desired.

Getting back to my sexual development though, I think it is significant that prior to that time, I had only one same-sex friend with whom I had any semblance of a close relationship. In looking back, I noticed that when I went over to his house, I wanted to play exclusively with him; I never wanted to include any of the other boys in our play. Could it have been that I was so starved for male attention that I could not bear the thought of anyone else vying for the attention that I wanted? Not that I would have known it then, but hindsight, as they say, is always 20/20.

This neediness must have driven people away. I didn't know it then, but I must have been so incredibly clingy that no one wanted to be around me. Thus, I became withdrawn in my loneliness, not in an overtly negative way, but simply in an aloof sort of way. My participation in extracurricular activities was largely cursory and superficial, which was probably my way of avoiding any kind of intimacy.

As I mentioned earlier, I was never particularly good at sports either. My lack of coordination caused me never to develop my athletic skills for fear of looking stupid. I was also very clumsy, which I later came realize was an anxiety reaction to a stress-filled house.

It is a true wonder and a sublime grace from God that I never broke a bone! I always missed the ball when it was thrown to me because I would shut my eyes and turn away, which I now know is a reflex reaction of someone who is physically abused. This accentuated my already below-average athletic abilities and made me disdain the world of team sports.

Adding to that, I am also deaf in both ears and wear hearing aids. Even with those, it was difficult for me to hear what was being said in open spaces or places with a lot of reverberations like the gym, which I didn't realize until very recently when my own son (who suffers my same genetic hearing

loss) had difficulty hearing the coaches when playing basketball. Boys (who can be cruel) would make fun of me for
that all the time.

It didn't help that a guy would say something to me and
I didn't respond because I didn't hear him. Because of this,
I often looked like I was stupid or "zoned out" because I
would ask people to repeat themselves or just not hear them,
even when they were speaking directly to me. The teasing
was merciless, and after a while, I just didn't want to deal
with the pain, so I avoided interactions with boys whenever
possible. A less sensitive boy would have probably joined in
the fun somehow, but that wasn't me.

Not that I was ever particularly enamored with sports
anyway, but unfortunately, most of the other boys were. It
is very painful to always be the last one picked to be on a
team. I remember those days during mandatory gym class
when teams were being selected and praying that just once I
wouldn't be the last one or two chosen.

It never happened that I can remember.

I was the zoned-out deaf kid with the hearing aids in the
corner that the unlucky team *had* to take.

My deafness didn't help me gain any foothold into any
other parts of the male world either. It so happened that the
tones I don't hear are low tones, not high ones. So I couldn't
hear the voices of most men, and since many men and boys
tend to mumble when they speak, it made it even worse.

It was never a problem in the classroom because I could
easily hear the high-pitched voices of women and girls. So for
me, trying to hear what men and boys were saying became

an exhausting task which was often met with ridicule from my peers, so I just stopped trying.

I was also not very much into other stereotypically masculine interests, like cars. By the time high school rolled around, I began to hear the boys talk about girls and women in very derogatory terms revolving around sexual conquests. I rightly rebelled against this but for the wrong reason, and I didn't really know about redeemed male culture and that there were boys (and men) who didn't think like that. Of course, how do boys label other boys who are not interested in sexual conquests?

Gay.

Faggot.

Queer.

Fairy.

This is probably what led, in part, to my further disenchantment with men and my embracing of feminine culture. Women seemed so much more kind and caring than men and they seemed to talk about *real* stuff, not just cars, sports, and sex. They had better stories. They were more interesting.

Ironically though, I always thought that I was somehow more mature and morally superior to my same-sex peers, yet always felt like a little kid around them. I can see now that I entertained a sort of ambivalence where I deeply desired friendship on the one hand but rejected them on the other.

Because of what I perceived as the roughness and crudeness of boys and how much hurt I felt at their hands, I actually preferred being with opposite-sex friends during adolescence.

I seemed to be able to relate better to girls and they didn't hurt me. I don't recall ever going through the "girls are yucky" stage that most boys go through. This, I told myself, was yet another sign of my "maturity." I didn't like playing with boys because I felt that they were "too rough."

Since my confidence was so low, I was not very physically aggressive, and the physical aggression of my male peers seemed all but appealing to me. I was constantly afraid of doing something "clumsy" that would attract their attention and bring ridicule on myself. I can remember some days when the ridicule was so bad that I dreaded coming into school. This was just another reason I was not "one of them," I told myself.

My physical appearance only confirmed that.

I hated my body.

I always felt awkward, thought I was too skinny, that my hips were too wide, that my voice was not deep enough, that I had a "chicken" chest, that I was too short, not muscular or hairy enough, appeared too girlish, and my genitals were too small.

Although I have a more accurate view of myself now, back then I had a "baby face" and maybe some feminine mannerisms to the point that I was even mistaken for a girl on more than one occasion.

Even today, although no one would ever mistake me for a woman in person, I am still occasionally called "ma'am" on the phone. I laugh about it now but hated everything about my physical appearance then and thought I was too "girly looking."

This was further reinforced because the hearing aids always made me feel really self-conscious and different from everyone else. So if my peers thought their assessments of me as a fag, wimp, and sissy were true, why not hang with the girls who wouldn't ridicule me or choose me last for teams?

Nonetheless, in spite of my dislike of the whole sporting thing and my self-consciousness about my body, I ended up playing on our basketball team in elementary school.

Boy, did I stink.

I kid you not that I scored only two points *per season*. It became a family joke after a while.

However, there was one thing I did learn from playing sports.

I was a very late-bloomer, so to speak, and I found myself really admiring the bodies of my larger, more well-developed peers. They already had the obvious growth spurts with the broad shoulders, body and facial hair, big muscles, and noticeably bigger genitals than mine.

What was happening? When would my penis grow, my shoulders broaden, and my muscles get bigger? I felt like a little boy in the presence of young men who were only a year or two older than I was. Surely, something was wrong with me!

Even as late as spring of 1996, when I was twenty-one and already in college, I still had not yet "filled out" into the body of a man. A journal entry from that time reads, "I still have half the body of a boy and half of a man. I am still fairly thin and my voice is just changing now. It still squeaks and everything like Peter Brady's. I think my 'late' blooming has a lot to do with my not pursuing women. I don't feel manly. Being gay, I know what masculinity looks like and I just don't have it."

I was different.

I was weird.

I was not like the other boys.

Big Men, the WWF, and the Bodybuilder in the Pasta Shop

When people hear my story, they very quickly figure out that I don't fit the typical mold. Even among the community of fellow SSA strugglers, most people can't figure me out. I admit that I even confuse myself at times. At first glance, my early childhood doesn't seem that different from most others. I mean, who wasn't bullied as a kid? Who didn't have problems fitting in? Can something like that actually turn a kid *gay*?

Some men who have left the gay lifestyle ask me if I am sure I was ever actually gay. Maybe I was just confused or maybe an unresolved bisexual man? On the opposite end of the spectrum, I once had a gay activist try to convince me that I was really gay and just needed to accept that and stop hating myself.

See what I mean? It's really hard to pin me down!

I don't blame people for getting frustrated with their inability to fit me into a neat, socially-constructed box.

So here it is.

For as long as I can remember, I have felt an affinity for and an attraction to men. Prior to puberty, this expressed itself as an admiration for handsome or strong men. As a child, when we would play "pretend" games where we assumed the role of the character from a show or other story, I always chose to be the good-looking or muscular guy.

I remember one time back in the third grade when we were playing *The A-Team* based on the popular '80s show. I always chose to be Faceman purely because I thought the actor, Dirk Benedict, was so handsome. No one ever fought me for the part.

The other boys were much more interested in playing the part of Hannibal, who was clearly the brains behind the outfit and de facto leader of the group. They might also lobby to play the mercurial B.A. Baracus, who solved most problems with his brute strength, or Howling Mad Murdoch, who despite his rather tenuous grasp on reality, was actually quite funny.

Not me. I wanted the good-looking guy. I wanted *to be* the good-looking guy.

Even before that, although I was never all that much into sports, my dad used to watch football. I watched too, but not because of the game. I loved looking at the players and their muscles rippling and bulging beneath their jerseys. They looked so strong, *so powerful.* Mind you, this was not yet a sexual thing; I was probably only five or six years old at the time, but those desires were already present, although latent.

Not long after that, I happened to be watching TV and a male bodybuilding competition came on. This was even better than football! Here was a bunch of almost nude bronzed men with huge, glistening muscles just flexing away for the world to admire. If I was capable of an erection at that point,

I definitely would have had one. I loved looking at their bodies and the larger-than-life muscularity. It made such an impression on me that even now, I can still remember those feelings of incredible awe. I couldn't stop looking!

There used to be this pasta shop by our house. I always looked forward to going because there was an autographed picture of a bodybuilder behind that counter who was apparently a friend of the owner. That picture was a feast for my eyes every time we went into that shop. It's a wonder that my parents never asked why I was always so eager to pick up the evening's spaghetti.

Probably not too many years after the discovery that I adored the male physique, I discovered that if I rubbed myself *down there*, it felt good. *Really good.*

Having no idea what was actually happening biologically, as this was well before "the talk" or the basic sex-ed of Catholic school, I would rub until I assumed what was a little bit of pee came out. I thought I had made the discovery of the ages. I mean, who else would figure this out? Even if someone did, who would actually *talk* about it?

With that came the realization that if I pretended certain things or had certain thoughts, my little budding manhood would rise up in acclamation. So, using blankets or stuffed animals stuffed into my PJs, I would make myself into one of those bodybuilders I so admired.

I flexed for my imaginary audience and imagined myself one of those big men. I felt great! Over time, as more and more testosterone flooded my body to begin the transition to manhood, I began to realize that my fantastical bigness also gave me bigness *down there*, and so began the process of sexualizing my admiration of men culminating in what I realize now were my first orgasms.

Eventually, I moved from stuffed animals and blankets to looking at the real thing on TV. Still, not entirely realizing the significance of what I was doing, I began looking at the bodybuilding competitions and doing the same thing while watching them.

Then I discovered professional wrestling.

I know I'm dating myself here, but back in the '80s, the main professional wrestling organization was called the WWF, not the WWE. I would watch the matches every Saturday morning and enjoy my "feel-good" time with myself.

Again, all this was kind of innocent. I was naïve and didn't fully understand what was happening or how wrong and, yes, *disordered* it was. I just know I liked it, and I liked looking at those men with their oiled and well-muscled bodies pounding against each other.

Eventually, I moved from the screen to real life. One summer, we had a boy from another state who was a friend of the family come to stay with us for the day. He was the nephew of a close friend of the family. He was physically more mature than me, tan and muscular, though not that much older than me. We swam in the pool together for most of the day.

We often wrestled in the water as boys do, and I really liked the feeling of his muscular body against mine. At one point, I got an erection and I know he felt it. It didn't concern me at the time as I still was pretty unaware of my own sexuality, but this was one of the few times that I had anything close to a sexual experience with a boy.

I didn't realize it at the time, but when I did, this experience would later confirm that I was sexually attracted to other boys. I began to realize at this point that something was not right with me. I was definitely not *normal*.

As those male hormones coursed through my body, my attractions to men began to intensify.

Then the fantasies began coming.

I discovered actual masturbation, and it became a new way for me to exercise my own imaginative powers and, at the same time, get some pleasurable feelings out of the deal. My homosexual fantasies became more and more intense, fueled by heterosexual "soft" pornography and men on TV. Masturbation quickly became an obsession. I did it anywhere and anytime I could, and my fantasies became more and more explicitly homosexual in nature.

This was something I did by myself. The only time I came even remotely close to experimenting with another boy was with one of my few elementary school classmates with whom I socialized.

One day when we were hanging out in his room, he got into his bed under his blanket. He suggested that we play a game wherein we rubbed each other's genitals through the comforter while we talked. It only happened once, and it never went beyond that. We actually never even discussed it again even though we remained friends a few years after that, but that incident must have served to further cement the eroticization of masculinity for me.

In a similar vein, at one point, as I began to develop physically, my cousin's boyfriend gave me a weight set to help develop my strength. Knowing this, and probably to encourage me in this area, one of my dad's friends, who always kept himself in great shape, gave me an old issue of a bodybuilding magazine.

Wow! A whole magazine of all-but-naked musclemen I could look at any time I wanted! I had hit pay dirt! And I certainly didn't keep the magazine just because I liked the articles. Did it even have articles in it? I didn't care. The magazine became for me what *Playboy* or *Penthouse* probably was for most boys my age. Even then, even though I knew this was wrong at some level, I still didn't really *get* it.

Fortunately, I was never really into hardcore porn. I've only ever seen it a handful of times. One of those times was when I worked at an auto body shop as the clean-up guy. The workers left a magazine in one of the drawers, and as I cleaned, I stumbled upon it. I never saw erections that size in my life! I was fascinated. I was *turned on*. There were naked women in those magazines too, but I only had eyes for those big men and their impressive manhoods.

Speaking of the boys my own age, as boys do, they began to talk about girls in sexual ways and their bodies. I was really not interested. I was kind of *repulsed* if the truth be told. I didn't want to think about women like that! I mean, I played the game and tried to join in the banter as best I could, but I just didn't understand what they were getting so excited about. What I was really interested in was looking at *them*, especially when they had their shirts off.

Finally, in one, horrific instant, it *dawned* on me and crashed down on me like a life-changing pile of bricks.

Holy cow. The feelings that these boys used to describe girls were the exact same feelings I would use to describe what happened when I saw an attractive man or boy. The thoughts and feelings and physical reactions *they* were describing about the opposite sex, I was having about *them*!

Now things were making sense, but what a terrifying realization.

That was the fateful day, during the summer right before high school, that I came to the conclusion that I was *gay*.

This was just such a foreign concept to me; it would have been akin to discovering after twelve years that I was black or Asian. I mean, that's how strange and incomprehensible it was to my naïve mind.

It *couldn't* be, I thought. No, not me.

With horror, I began to piece my life together with what I knew about what it was supposed to be like to be gay. The pieces fit. I gradually accepted that it must be so.

It was so hard to accept; I couldn't really be *gay*, could I? There.

I had said it, the g-word.

All those boys were right about me. They must have seen something I couldn't.

It was one neat label which I could affix to myself in order to make sense of why everything seemed so screwed up. I had always felt different and this explained why. I was different. I was, as the word sums up, *queer*.

I was *gay*.

The Male and Female
Ends of Things

"Is that the male end or the female end?" my dad asked me one day as we tried to assemble a toy I had been given.

I looked at it and seeing that it had a part sticking out, I said without hesitation, "Oh, it's the male end."

I knew that the female part would be the one that the male part fit into to join and fuse whatever object we had been assembling into one functional unit. It was intuitive. Two bolts together are unable to be attached and serve no useful purpose. The same with two wingnuts.

Useless.

It made perfect sense to me. That didn't translate into my own experience though.

Even though I now had a word to describe myself and that feeling of being "different" all my life, I didn't really know what that meant. I knew that gay men were men who liked other men the way most men like women. I was one of *those* guys.

By this point, I also had a basic knowledge of the "birds and the bees," and my parents were always very honest about how babies were made and how the male and female anatomy went together to produce babies. It just made perfect sense, just like bolts and wingnuts.

So I was genuinely puzzled. If I liked men and I were to have sex with men, where would I put my "male end"? From my point of view, there didn't seem to be any possible way it would work out. As I said before, I was still kind of on the naïve end of the spectrum, so one day, I actually asked my dad how gay men have sex.

He stopped moving the pool ladder he was wrestling into place and said very bluntly, "They either suck on each other's penises or they stick them into each other's heinies."

I must have had such a horrified look on my face that he burst out laughing.

"Yup," he continued. "That's how it's done, son. You put it in another man's poop. That doesn't sound like much fun does it?"

Fun?

No. It was absolutely disgusting, even *revolting*.

Satisfied that he had elicited the desired reaction in me, Dad went back to his pool ladder.

I, on the other hand, was still reeling. I could understand the mouth thing maybe, but in the butt? It took a while to wrap my brain around that one. So I desired men sexually, but the only way to make it work was *that* way? I wasn't so sure I could handle that.

Back then, being gay was still pretty much a closeted thing and was just starting to be accepted by mainstream society as an "alternative" lifestyle. The thought of being involved in that lifestyle and giving full vent to these overwhelming feelings was extremely alluring and at the same time depressing.

At that moment, I began to lose hope.

All my dreams of what my life would be were suddenly dashed to pieces. I had always imagined myself getting married and having children, a nice house and maybe even a dog. It was the American Dream, the hope of humanity.

Nope. Not for me.

I was trapped between my desire for a "normal" heterosexual life and my very real desire for, attraction to, and even, at times, *obsession* with men.

Just weeks away from starting high school, I felt as if I had lost everything. What was left for me?

At that moment, I decided that no one would ever know my dirty little secret. I would keep it safely hidden and carry it with me to the grave. It was too shameful and only meant to be shared between God and myself since he had inflicted this on me, or so I thought. This cross, I had decided, I would carry alone. Little did I know that the weight of it would nearly destroy me.

I decided to get on with life and just pretend this thing wasn't there. I had no intention of ever "consummating" my gay identity, because despite my feelings, I knew deep down inside that homosexual acts or, indeed, any sexual act outside of marriage were not God's will. Suffering through life with these unwanted but all-consuming desires seemed to me to be exactly what God had in store for me.

That tyrant.

Not that I would have voiced it then, but my discovery of my homosexuality began to drive a wedge, however small, between me and my Creator that day. The wedge would one day become a chasm that the Mother of Jesus herself would need to cross to bring me back to him.

I didn't want those feelings and desires, so I hid, rather than face them. I went on with my double-life, determined to show the world a publicly "normal" guy with no problems while I privately engaged in my dark fantasies. Eventually, I began to fantasize even about things I had found loathsome before.

Although I never had physical sex with a man, Jesus says clearly in Matthew 5:28, "I say to you, everyone who looks at a woman [read *man*] with lust has already committed adultery with her [read *him!*] in his heart."

As I progressed through high school, these fantasies began to have a greater and greater hold on me. As is the way with all sin, once it has become entrenched, it turns the person in on himself and away from communion with others. Thus, being alone started to become that which I valued most in life. I just wanted to read books or watch TV and be by myself so no one would ever discover my secret darkness.

I wasn't super involved in high school beyond the social events that *everyone* went to. I posed for my prom pictures (my dates were always "just friends"), went to the National Honor Society Induction, and excelled academically, but that was the end of it. I didn't make very many lasting friendships.

I ran on the track team but never really put my heart into it. I never got to know the other guys on my team or partook of any of the social events of team life, like the regular pasta parties at one team member or another's house.

I just did not want to let any of those guys (some of whom were probably really *nice guys*) see who I really was. I felt like a little boy trying to navigate the world of young men (many of whom I was sexually attracted to). It was just too much for me to handle. It wasn't *safe*.

This even extended into my freshman year at college when I declined to live at school, opting to stay at home for my first two years, thereby missing all the shared experiences that entailed. Eventually, I started feeling loneliness and a strong desire for companionship. It was then that a profound sense of isolation settled on me.

The pain was intense, and I self-medicated through fantasy and masturbation, as many SSA men do. I felt like such a loser and like a total failure as a man. I wanted some man to come and save me from myself. Although the reason I fantasized about having sex with men was to make me feel like more of a man, it ultimately had the opposite effect. I felt like a little boy masquerading as a man and began to see girls more like women that I would never be man enough to have.

As a result, I became more and more comfortable believing the lie that I was gay and thus had no hope for a significant heterosexual relationship. This shielded me from all the responsibility, heartache, and heartbreak of even trying to date women. I simply excused myself through my sexual orientation.

None of the girls I liked were ever interested in me, so I figured I must not be interesting to women. I was not a "real" man. Why would any woman want me for more than a "friend"? Surely, I was not capable of being a woman's lover.

Although I was never "out," I must have been seen as the weird, closeted gay dude who hung around with the girls.

Without going into graphic detail, I will tell you that if we take the Lord at his Word regarding that passage from Matthew—and we *should*—then I confess that I was one of the greatest perpetrators of sexual sin. There is not much perversity in which I did not partake in my heart.

I know now that beyond a shadow of a doubt, if I had ever pursued the gay lifestyle, I would have explored all avenues. You name it, I've done it, desired it, and *liked* it all at one point, at least in my heart and mind. I *wanted* a man to have his way with me; it was an aching hole that I longed to have filled.

There was *nothing* about the gay lifestyle that I didn't find thrilling at some level (even if it was at the same time *revolting*) at one point or another. I know the darkness of my own soul and the depth of my own sexual sins, and I just thank the Lord Jesus and his Blessed Mother for entering that darkness and saving me from being eternally lost.

Jesus Christ was the man who came *to save me from myself.*

The Year Good Friday Came Early

The time after I graduated high school was one of the hardest and most painful times of my life. I was a twenty-year-old college sophomore. Recall that up until this point, I had never shared my struggle with anyone, so I had been carrying this cross alone for all of my pre-teen and teen years.

I prayed, I went to Mass, I went to confession, I talked to God regularly, and although there were moments of respite, the cross did not appear to get lighter but rather heavier.

I struggled with it daily and tried to be mindful of the Lord's blessings, but I felt so alone and miserable that I really didn't understand how I could endure all that pain. Humanly speaking, it is impossible. That's why it's good that it didn't depend on my humanity but rather on the power of the Risen Lord.

I was so consumed by my suffering, pain, and shame that I began succumbing to the darkness and walling myself off from other people. I was so angry at God for having made me this way (or so I thought then) that I took all my pain out on him and started to lose my faith and my hope.

However, in my smallness of mind, I continued unnecessarily martyring myself for the sake of what I knew was right. I asked God to fix me, but it seemed like all my cries to heaven fell on deaf ears.

Nothing was changing.

Going to a public college didn't help. I was bombarded on what seemed like all sides with messages telling me that it was "OK to be gay" and, "Homosexuality is not the problem. Homophobia is," as the signs posted all around campus proclaimed.

Likewise, there was a fairly active gay presence on campus, and many (probably well-intentioned) professors encouraged us to explore those "alternative" lifestyles. The message that was coming through loud and clear was that if I was gay, I should accept it, embrace it, and have a great time.

I was assured that I'd be happy if I did and miserable if I didn't.

It seemed fairly accurate. Here I was, gay and not sexually active with men, and feeling, as promised, absolutely miserable.

I poured my misery out in another journal entry from around that time:

> I hate being gay. I would love to have a boyfriend and be sexually active. Just the thought of being naked with another man thrills me. I love everything about men: their bodies, their looks, their smells . . . everything. How I wish I could get with another man and explore his body with my hands, feel his muscles and his genitals. I wonder what his hairy skin would feel like against mine? I wish I could feel this kind of longing for women. It's so upsetting. I wish I could change this but I'm not hopeful. Should I remain in

the Church or pursue my homosexual interests? I'm
here for now but it gets harder by the day.

In my view, God was nowhere to be found. He seemed
more and more distant with each passing day. Happiness
seemed all around me, just not at my door. If I had to pick
one word to describe this time in my life, it would be *lonely*.

This is ironic because there were people around me all the
time.

My family, although they did not know anything of my
inner turmoil, was one place where I always felt safe. I always
enjoyed our holiday gatherings with the extended family
or just quiet dinners at home with my parents and sister.
I really had very few friends, and the few I had, I certainly
wouldn't confide in. What would they think? What would
my parents think?

At the time, I didn't realize this, but rather than face this
pain and loneliness, I buried myself in my activities. Since
I lived at home, I would do all my homework during my
down times on campus so I could be free to read or do other
activities at home. I guess since I felt so safe at home, I would
most rather have been there. Even that wasn't the consolation it once was. I journaled this:

> I have no one. Who can I talk to? Who would under-
> stand? It seems that my whole support system is falling
> apart. I don't feel the same affection for my parents
> that I once did, nor is my extended family what I
> thought or idealized them to be.

The problem was that I really needed friends my own age, especially male friends, and I needed to put myself in places where I could start to make those connections.

Again, hindsight is always 20/20.

If I knew then what I know now, I certainly would have behaved differently.

How could I expect to grow with my peers if I never interacted with any? I was too afraid of my own secrets getting out to seek any friends. Thus, in a vicious cycle, my pain continued through my self-imposed Catch-22.

It seems so obvious now, but then, I was blinded by my own inwardness. I was paralyzed by fear. And fear is always the work of the devil. He had me right where he wanted me, the place where God never intended for anyone to be: *alone*. Even as far back as Genesis 2:18, God created humans to be in communion with one another.

My faith began to crumble away as I slipped into despair. It finally came to a head over winter break that year.

I hit rock bottom.

I had nothing left.

So I thought.

He was about to do something wonderful in my life that was going to give him glory and begin my journey of healing and wholeness. But I digress; before I talk about my Easter Sunday, I have to finish talking about my Good Friday, which came early that year, at least for me.

It began in the middle of January 1996. It was a brisk, January weekend, the last one before classes resumed for the spring session. I was always very involved on campus in the leadership of various high-profile organizations. It must have been part of my avoidance, because I made very few close friends through any of them.

Because of my involvement in these organizations, I was invited back to campus early in order to participate in a retreat-like workshop on diversity. Now, anyone who has been involved in public or higher education knows that people who identify as gay are considered minorities who, like any other minority group, are to be accepted under the banner of "diversity." I fully expected that this would be included in the agenda for the day, but I had no idea that this was the day the Lord had chosen for me to end my isolation.

Quite frankly, I really don't remember much of the day or the details surrounding it. What I do remember is that the presenter was a guy from a gay-advocacy organization in New York whose mission it was to foster *acceptance*, not just tolerance, of everyone and his or her lifestyle choices.

He was an excellent speaker. He was a very masculine-looking, muscular guy who seemed very comfortable with himself. I had the shock of my life when at the end of his presentation, he revealed himself as gay. This just about shattered my whole stereotype-fed worldview about gay men.

There's this thing in psychology called cognitive dissonance. It means that if a person tries to hold conflicting viewpoints or beliefs simultaneously, the human mind cannot tolerate contradiction, so one will eventually win out over the other.

For me, the tension of my cognitive dissonance peaked at that moment. I had the epitome of what the world and the college taught right in front of me: an attractive, likeable, seemingly confident man who had identified as gay and was proud of it.

He even went so far as to say that he hated it when people said that it was "such a waste that he was gay." He didn't believe it was a waste at all. He said that he loved being gay and all that it entailed.

On the other side of my cognitive dissonance was the ever more distant voice of Jesus Christ and his Church, who told me that ultimate happiness was not possible if I chose a gay lifestyle and that if I remained faithful to the Gospel, joy would be mine.

I was ready jump off Saint Peter's Boat right then and there. Screw Jesus and the Gospel, I thought. Here I am, miserable and lonely while this guy has a partner who loves him and a happy life waiting at home.

Finally, things became too much for me to handle. At that instant, seven years of emotional pain wracked my body at once. I was now rocked with physical pain that seemed to reach every part of my body; my stomach was twisted in knots, my head pounded, and my shoulders felt like they were in the grip of a vise. Even my heart seemed to throb in pain with each beat.

I had to get this out.

I could no longer remain silent.

I uttered a desperate prayer between sobs for God to show me the way.

He *was* listening.

The Lord visited me that day in the person of the campus priest named Father Dave. Father Dave and I had been friends at that point for about two years. I had worked with him closely through my involvement with the Catholic Campus Ministry at the college. I wouldn't say he was the most orthodox of priests, but it was very clear that he loved ministering to college students.

He was very gifted at meeting people in whatever circumstances they presently found themselves, and this is probably one of the things that built trust between us, because that was an area in which I still needed to grow.

It is so ironic that priests, even the good ones, are so attacked today as being "homophobic" and "uncompassionate," yet it was to a priest that I went to share my deep, dark secret. I had no idea what kind of a reaction I was going to get, but somehow I knew I could share this with Father Dave—I had to, the cross was getting too heavy to bear alone.

It came about in a strange way. As soon as the talk was over, I tried to call Father several times. He lived in a house just off campus; the first floor was kind of a common area while the upstairs was the priest's apartment. Much to my chagrin, he did not answer his phone.

So I got in my car and drove by his house. Upon noticing his car in the driveway, I figured I might as well give it a shot, so I turned the car around into the driveway and knocked.

A wheezing, sickly-looking Father Dave answered the door. The poor man looked like death warmed over. His salt-and-pepper hair served to highlight his sickly pale face. I immediately felt guilty for having disturbed him. In any case, he greeted me and I asked him if he had time to see me.

"Sure, c'mon in," he nasally intoned as he wiped his bright-red, runny nose.

I don't think I ever remember Father Dave turning anyone away in all the years that I knew him. It is this kind of selfless dedication to which God calls all Christians in whatever state of life they happen to be and which was so well exemplified by this wonderful priest. It was kind of fortunate for me that Father was ill because then I couldn't beat around the bush. I had to get right to the point. So I did it. For the first time in my life, I dropped the G-bomb on someone.

"Father, I have something I need to share with you. . . . I'm *gay*," I said.

I let the seven-year secret spill out and then probably winced as I waited to see what Father would say. Because of all the horror stories the media put out there, I half-expected Father to throw me out of there or at least seem a little uncomfortable, although I knew in my heart that Father Dave was not that kind of guy. He didn't even flinch. He just nodded his head slightly.

"Yes. Go on," he said.

"I've never told anyone this before," I continued.

"Thank you for trusting me," he answered.

"I really don't know what to do now. What do I do? I mean, I know I can't act on it . . ." I asked.

At that point, all the years of pain came pouring out. I told him of my struggles and my anger with God and that I did not understand why God would make me gay if I could not act on it. Indeed, from that logic, the gay rights movement makes a lot of sense. At that point, I was still firmly convinced that being gay was not something I could change no matter how hard I prayed or how much therapy I received.

Father was really understanding. The Lord truly sent this priest to minister to me in my hour of need. Again, the enormity of what was happening here was not completely obvious at the time, but I would grow into understanding much later on. In between wheezes and sniffles, Father managed to give me a big hug and thank me for trusting him with my suffering.

He very gently affirmed the Church's teaching on homosexual acts as intrinsically wrong and told me that I was called to a life of chastity, and possibly celibacy, but that the real test of my character was in what I did with this cross. He told me that God had a plan, that I had a very fulfilling life ahead of me and that I need not despair.

He continued, "You always have a friend to talk to if you need to."

I then asked him to allow me to make my confession, and I remember feeling relief after receiving the blessing, "I absolve you from your sins in the Name of the Father and the Son and the Holy Spirit. Go in peace."

So I went in peace, at least for a while.

Father Dave became a close confidante of mine. I went to see him whenever I felt burdened by this cross, and he was always there for me.

But, although I was no longer alone, there were still many questions on my heart. I still didn't understand why I was this way, why I was so different, why so many people could live a happily married life and I couldn't. I tried my best to live a faith-filled life although my struggle was tearing me apart inside. If I had a relationship with God, then why did

I feel so broken? I went to Mass every Sunday and confession regularly, even daily Mass on occasion. What was missing?

The answer is Jesus Christ. It wasn't that I didn't have a relationship with him, because I believe I always did. Nor was it that I didn't trust him. I did.

At least I *thought* I did.

But I didn't really ever put him in the very center of my life in order to realize just who he is and what he can do. Like millions of Christians today, I had unknowingly robbed Christ's holy cross of its power.

Quite simply, I didn't know Jesus knew me. I knew that I knew him, but once I realized that the Sovereign Lord and Master of the Universe, the Commander of the Heavenly Host and the Great I AM knew me and cared specifically about me, it changed everything.

This saving knowledge was mediated to me by none other than the Mother of God herself in what was once a sleepy little Portuguese village called Fatima, but I would have to endure more suffering and pain before receiving those graces.

A Future Saint and "Kisses"
From Our Lady

I mentioned earlier that my grandmother had instilled the Catholic Faith in my heart back when I was a little child and she had also introduced me to devotion to the Virgin Mary, who has always been very present in my life, even during those times that God seemed so far away. It was ultimately through her intercession that Jesus Christ healed me, but it was a long and difficult journey that would bring me to Fatima. Before Our Lady would bring me to her great shrine, she would periodically send me little "kisses" along the way just to let me know she was still there.

She was the one who always kept me on the right path even when I fought her kicking and screaming. Were it not for her gracious advocacy for me with her Divine Son, I would surely have been lost. I have no doubt about that. My little secret was hidden safely away from prying eyes, but I had imprisoned myself in my own loneliness, allowing no visitors to my tortured soul. Gradually, this loneliness gave way more directly to anger at God, whom I perceived to be the cause of my malady.

Why would God give me these painful and sometimes consuming passions only to forbid me to act on them? Why did he persist in his torture of me? What did he want? I had already resolved not to seek a sinful path. Why then couldn't God leave me alone? I struggled so hard. I knew in my heart what was right. Why this awful conflict? I hated myself. Why was I like this?

Some days it wasn't so bad. I could almost endure. Sometimes I forgot my trouble entirely. Other days were especially difficult, particularly those when I was put into situations where I saw men living the "gay lifestyle" who seemed happy enough and genuinely seemed to enjoy the life they were leading and each other. They seemed happy and I was so very miserable and lonely. I was so desperate for that love from a man that it caused me an almost physical pain. Thus, the wedge driven between my soul and its Master grew deeper. Although I never stopped going to Mass or receiving the sacraments, especially confession, I began to lose my faith. I felt that God had left me and was far from my sorry situation.

At one point, I was in so much pain and consumed by so much anger that I shook my fist at the Lord and shouted, "Damn you and damn your Church! I want nothing to do with you!"

As soon as I said it, I interiorly heard Our Lady ask, "And damn *me* too?"

No. Not *you*, I thought.

Not *her*.

And if I was staying with *her*, that meant I also had to stay with *him*, even though I didn't like *him* very much at that point, even though he kept calling out to me in the darkness.

One of the most profound consolations I can remember is meeting with the visionary of Betania, Venezuela, Maria

Esperanza de Bianchini. *Betania*—Spanish for *Bethany,* the biblical town from which Saints Lazarus, Mary, and Martha hailed—is a twentieth-century site of apparitions of the Virgin Mary, approved by the local bishop, though not yet by the Vatican. After visiting the shrine, thousands of people claimed to have been healed of maladies such as cancer and AIDS and countless others. Many people besides Maria Esperanza also report having seen the Virgin Mary walking the grounds there.

Maria herself was not what I expected in a visionary with such profound spiritual gifts. She was a stylish, attractive matriarch who wore makeup, had her hair done, and dressed well. She appeared to be quite cosmopolitan and traveled with her husband and an entourage of her children and their spouses and even some of her grandchildren. She had a warm, infectious smile and a serene manner which put all those around her at ease.

Although from an American perspective it was somewhat surprising to see how many of her family members traveled with her, it really fit right in with her message about the importance of family, a message which is even more sorely needed today.

I even had a chance to speak with her daughter Maria Grazia (all of Maria's daughters are named after the blessed Virgin, with different middle names) who described Our Lady to me as she had witnessed her one day on the grounds of Betania. Noting that she was beautiful beyond description, Maria Grazia said she looked like a nun as the breeze blew her veil. Clearly, there was a lot going on in Betania!

Maria Esperanza had been invited by my pastor to give a talk. The church was packed that evening and many people were waiting in line to have Maria pray over them after her talk. Our pastor reported that over two thousand hosts were distributed at communion! While I would have liked to have been prayed over, there was no urgent need on my part since I didn't really think she could help me, yet somehow we ended up staying in church well after Mass.

One of the reasons is my aforementioned deafness. Since toddlerhood, I have been almost completely deaf in my left ear and moderately deaf in my right. Despite having numerous corrective surgeries performed by the best doctors in the world over the years, I never got my hearing back. I have worn hearing aids since I was in second grade, and I had more or less reconciled myself to wearing hearing aids for the rest of my life.

It really didn't even bother me that much anymore, but in my small parish, everyone was well aware of the problem and we had attended many healing services in the past in hopes of restoration. I think everyone else wanted it more than I did. I had other more burdensome things in my heart from which I was seeking healing.

So we waited.

After six hours had passed, it was time for Maria to retire and somehow (I'm still not quite sure how), my parents and I ended up escorting her to the rectory where she was staying. As I walked behind her, I noticed that she wore a beautiful scent which smelled like roses. I ended up in the living room of the rectory along with Maria, her husband, her translator, my parents, and my pastor. The next thing I knew, Father was explaining to Maria's translator that I had suffered hearing loss and asked if she would pray over me.

Despite the fact that she was ready to retire for the night, once the translator explained what Father was asking for, Maria Esperanza turned and looked at me with an intense and penetrating gaze that I will never forget and smiled the most beautiful smile.

She looked right through me.

She took my folded hands in hers and began talking to me through her translator. Just being in her presence enveloped me in a sense of peace which was enhanced by the smell of the wonderful perfume she was wearing. She closed her eyes and prayed silently, waiting for the Lord to speak to her. Finally, her eyes opened. She tightened her grip on my hands and again looked deeply into my own eyes as she said, "*Paciencia, paciencia y más paciencia.*"

"Patience, patience, and more patience."

"Sometimes," she said through her translator, "God permits things that we don't understand, but we always have to trust in him."

Among her many spiritual gifts—which included levitation, bilocation, the stigmata, and miraculous communions—Maria also had the gift of "reading hearts." This simply means that the Lord granted to her the ability to understand people's motivations, thoughts, and feelings so that she could effectively minister to them. It is not mind reading, as the conscience is the area of a person reserved to God and that person alone, but it certainly gives the gifted person deeper insight than most other people.

She closed her eyes and prayed again. When she opened them, I knew that she had seen my struggle. She smiled and began describing my life in ways that only she and I would understand. Although I don't remember everything she said, one thing was certain: healing would not happen tonight, either of my hearing or my homosexuality.

What was so interesting is that she laid her hands on and prayed over everyone I saw in church that night. She did not lay her hands on me. It was as if she knew God's will at this time. My pastor and family thought that all she said and did referred only to my hearing. Maria and I knew differently.

On the way home, I thought God's answer to my prayer for healing of homosexuality appeared to be no.

Yet, I was not disconsolate or depressed about this. Rather, I felt strangely comforted, especially since the smell that I had so loved on Maria Esperanza was now on my own hands. It was so strong that I smelled my hands during the whole ride home and again as I went to sleep. When I woke the next morning, the scent was still there, although not as strong. Even after showering, the scent still largely remained. It took three days, as I recall, for the scent to completely disappear.

Imagine my surprise and joy when I found out several months later that one of Maria Esperanza's other spiritual gifts is that she exuded the "odor of sanctity" in the form of the smell of roses. I was even more awed when I further discovered that objects she touched also took on the smell!

While this may seem kind of strange, it was even more surprising that my parents, who had been in just as close proximity to Maria, said they smelled nothing. Our Lady had again left her mark upon me through a woman who had been blessed to gaze upon her in person and converse with her. I came to see the smell of roses on my hands as yet another "kiss" of consolation from Our Lady through the person of Maria Esperanza, who resembled the Mother of Jesus to me in so many ways. What a grace!

Mary Hope is the English translation of Maria Esperanza's name. Maria indeed conveyed the message of her name. Many of the gifts that Maria Esperanza had were very similar to those of the popular Italian saint Padre Pio of Pietrelcina, including the ability to read hearts.

Hope.

The Lord provided me with the gift of hope through her, even though I was not yet ready for healing.

Mary Hope.

Mary and the virtue of hope, those were the two gifts that were given to me through this little Venezuelan grandmother.

Jesus said to his beloved John in his dying gasps, "Behold your mother."

Jesus gave his own mother to be our Mother in him through grace. It was *Mary* who was giving me (and countless others) *hope*.

I never met Maria Esperanza again, as she died of stomach cancer years later. Ironically, although she was Venezuelan, she had apparently returned to New Jersey for medical care where she died on August 7, 2004. From priests I know who had the grace of ministering to her on her deathbed, all sorts of manifestations of God's glory abounded in the room to the point that attending doctors and nurses would leave the room in shock after witnessing the phenomena asking, "Who *is* that woman?"

My brief encounter with Maria was meant to prepare me for my own encounter with Our Lady.

On January 31, 2010, Bishop Paul Bootkowski of the diocese of Metuchen, New Jersey, formally proclaimed Maria to have lived a life of heroic virtue and granted her the title Servant of God. Her cause for beatification and canonization has been opened and awaits action from the Congregation for the Causes of Saints in Rome.

"My Immaculate Heart Will Be Your Refuge"

When Our Lady appeared for the second time at Fatima on June 13, 1917, the children asked the blessed Virgin to take them to heaven. She assured them that Jacinta and Francisco would be taken "soon" but that Lucia would have to remain on earth for an indefinite period. Upon seeing Lucia's sadness at the prospect, Our Lady consoled her with these words, "Are you suffering a great deal? Do not lose heart. I will never forsake you. My immaculate heart will be your refuge and the way that will lead you to God."[15]

It was as if these words were meant for me. What had begun that January day at college simply intensified over the next year. I was in increasing emotional pain with each passing day. Then, when I simply could not go on anymore, Our Lady brought me to her great shrine in Portugal.

How I ended up in Fatima is purely due to the Providence of God and the special intercession of Our Lady. There is just no other explanation. Even now, it still seems incredible. In 1995, I entered a "contest" sponsored a Catholic apostolate which ran pilgrimages to various holy sites around the world.

---

15   World Apostolate of Fatima, USA, "June 13, 1917."

In 1995, the organization planned a 1996 pilgrimage to the Portuguese shrines, centered around the Basilica of Our Lady of Fatima. That year, they were trying something new. With the support of numerous benefactors, they were offering free pilgrimages for youth and young adults. The only requirement was that applicants had to send an essay and photo to the organization. The folks at the apostolate would then pray over and discern the applications seeking direction from God on which applicants he wished to send to Fatima.

Since I had always felt very close to the Virgin Mary throughout my life, even in those times when I didn't feel very close to Jesus, I welcomed the opportunity to go and experience a pilgrimage in a foreign country. So I filled out my essay (I guess it was late summer of 1995), sent it in, and forgot about it.

This time roughly corresponded to the year when I began to confide in Father Dave. It was a definite year of ups and downs. Some days were tolerable; others were really bad. I again started to lapse into depression and moodiness to the point where others around me began to notice. I must have been a real handful. I'm so grateful for the patience of my family during this time. Obviously, they had no idea what was going on inside me.

They say that to understand God's love for you, you need to hit what the psychologists and spiritual writers call "rock-bottom." This is when a person is brought so low that things seem hopeless. There is no strength left, no will left. The person is powerless and paralyzed. It is the point when a person is totally aware of their own helplessness and the moment that calls for change because life, the way it is, can no longer go on.

A decision must be made.

I thought I had done that after the diversity speaker at college. I didn't think it was possible to sink any lower than that.

Again, I was wrong. When I "bottomed out" at college, I wasn't really at the bottom. In fact, it was just another step, and with the support of Father Dave, I actually coped with it to a certain degree. The problem was, the essential question of my identity as a man was still unresolved. It was this nagging question that still haunted me and consumed me.

All this came to a head on the other side of the world, in the "land down-under." One of the things I had been blessed to enjoy was family trips. My parents did a terrific job with this. They made sure that my sister and I traveled the country and the world in order to be exposed to as many cultures and ways of life as possible. I will always be grateful for those wonderful times, and thanks to them, I am, as they say, *well-traveled*.

That particular year, we decided to travel to Australia together. It is an amazing place, so different from so many other places I've seen. The people were wonderful and the sights were amazing. We saw kangaroos and penguins in the wild, took in the city sights of Sydney and Melbourne and traveled to various national parks and preserves within that great country.

We even snorkeled on the Great Barrier Reef where the coral grows like trees. It was a dream vacation—the trip of a lifetime.

And I was miserable inside.

Don't get me wrong; I was really thrilled to be there, but I was so uncomfortable with myself and so lonely that it colored all the experiences with gray-tinted lenses.

One experience, in particular, shook me to my core. While we were in Sydney, we visited a section of town known as King's Cross. It was, as I remember it, a cross between Greenwich Village and how 42nd Street used to be in Manhattan before Rudolph Giuliani cleaned it up, with hints of Fremont Street of Las Vegas and Bourbon Street of New Orleans.

Despite a seedy, sexual undertone, King's Cross has a certain charm which attracts a lot of what we would call "artsy" folks. It also attracts a large gay community. Back then, it was even more open than anything I had seen in other cities, including New York. I guess the closest thing I could compare it to is San Francisco.

So, obviously, the streets of King's Cross were filled with gay lovers holding hands or walking arm-in-arm looking just euphoric with happiness. My heart was filled with longing, just to be understood and accepted and cared for by another man. I was sad, jealous, and lonely all at the same time. I knew something had to give.

I uttered one last desperate prayer to the Blessed Virgin. I wasn't speaking to the Lord at this point—I was too angry at him for what I thought he was doing to me. In essence, I later learned that I was always aware of his majesty and glory, just unable to relate to him as my Father. I still believed in him, I was just mad at him.

Anyway, I distinctly remember praying the following prayer to Our Lady, "Help me. I can't go on any more. Show me the way."

Our Lady's answer came in the mail in late spring of 1996 (actually before we left for Australia) when a large envelope arrived. By then that "contest" was so far from my mind that I couldn't imagine what the envelope could contain.

To my surprise, I found that I was one of about twenty young adults who would be given an all-expense-paid pilgrimage to Our Lady's Shrine in Portugal. It was the largest "prize" I had ever "won," only it wasn't really a prize at all—it was really a gift from the Queen of the Angels herself.

Of this, I have no doubt. I felt her hand in all of this.

As Saint John Paul II credited the Virgin Mary of Fatima with saving his life from an assassin's bullet in 1981, so do I credit that same august queen with saving me from myself and the "bullet" of the devil's whispers. Truly Our Lady of Fatima saved my life and brought me to the saving knowledge and healing power of Christ Jesus as only a mother could.

Yup. That's it. I just wrote an essay and ended up as a guest of heaven's queen in Portugal.

Crazy, huh?

But that's how it happened. I never took that blessing lightly; for me, it is the symbol of God's saving grace.

Did I deserve it?

No.

Were there other people out there more worthy than I?

Definitely.

Yet, she wanted *me*. Why?

There is no such thing as "cheap grace."

Our Lady wanted something from me.

She would reveal her purposes later on.

So after I returned from Australia with my family, it was time to pack up and head for Portugal by myself. Looking back, I see this as my first step towards manhood. I was truly a pilgrim, going to a strange and foreign land where I did not know the language or the customs with a group of people whom I did not know, away from my parents and everything I knew and held dear.

At one point very close to my departure, my Dad suddenly became skittish, and honestly, being a father now, I can understand why. It was all too good to be true. He began thinking about it and expressing his doubts about my going.

He wondered if this was some crazy cult and if I would be whisked away and never seen again. Seriously. And this was in the days *before* sex trafficking was so widely reported in the news! I grew a little bit nervous myself, quite honestly, but I knew in the depths of my heart that I *needed to* do this.

Add to that the Flight 800 accident where all 230 people onboard a trans-Atlantic flight to Paris perished as their plane exploded twelve minutes after takeoff from JFK Airport, from which I would be departing!

I was now officially afraid.

The Lord had stripped everything away and I was walking alone. I had nothing except the Blessed Virgin. I walked through that dark valley in pain, alone, afraid, and confused because of my self-imposed exile.

When I boarded that Trans-Air Portugal plane at JFK Airport, I somehow knew that I was leaving an old life behind.

I didn't know exactly how, but I knew God was working in me. What I experienced was beyond my wildest dreams.

He was there across the Atlantic waiting for me.

The Woman and the Dragon

After my red-eye across the Atlantic, I stepped off the plane in Lisbon. I felt very strange and it wasn't just the jet-lag. It was kind of like anxiety and tension but it really wasn't. I can't explain it except to say that it felt like a spiritual turmoil from within. Somehow I knew at that moment that there was a battle going on for my soul. The feeling was kind of intermittent and abated when our bus finally passed by the shining white Basilica of Our Lady of Fatima. It was an image I had seen many times before on television, and it was kind of surreal to see it in person.

It was near dusk when we got off the bus and a dry, warm breeze blew through the basilica's colonnade. I instantly felt a calming presence throughout my body. Everything seemed to slow down. The "anxiety" was gone, replaced by a sense of warmth and peace. It was so quiet there at sundown that day; the few pilgrims left were moving about slowly, praying and meditating.

As the sun set, the bells began to peal sharply to the tune of the old French hymn from Lourdes, known in English as "Immaculate Mary." I can still hear those bells and remember the comfort they brought that night and the whole time I was there. I was home in this oasis of peace in the House of Christ and the loving embrace of his Holy Mother.

When the sun rose over Portugal the next day, I couldn't help but be drawn to Our Lady's magnificent basilica with that golden statue of Christ in the center, his hands outstretched. There was something so peaceful and the stucco walls reflected the warm glow of the sunrise. It was such a pervasive peace that it was almost impossible to walk quickly on that hallowed ground. You just *had* to slow down.

Throughout the plaza are numerous images, statues, and various artifacts. One of the ones I remember is a small shrine wherein is encased a rather large chunk of the Berlin Wall. It is a living testimony to the power of Jesus Christ and the intercession of the Virgin Mary.

One of the more controversial components of Our Lady's apparitions at Fatima is her request that the pope consecrate Russia to her, promising world peace as a result. Indeed, after being nearly killed by a bullet from an assassin on the feast or Our Lady of Fatima on May 13, 1981, Pope St. John Paul II did, in fact, in consecrate the world (implicitly Russia) to Our Lady in union with all the bishops of the world three years later. Even though there is still controversy about whether the consecration was done exactly according to Our Lady's wishes, nonetheless, by the end of 1991, the Soviet Union had crumbled, not with a bang, but with a whimper.[16]

Our Lady's intercession here is undeniable. Consider all the dates of the significant events of the fall of the Soviet Union that year. The coup attempt against Mikhail Gorbachev, in which Soviet hard-liners attempted to take back

---

[16]   World Apostolate of Fatima, USA, "July 13, 1917."

control of Russia was defeated on August 22, the Feast of the Queenship of Mary. The Soviet Union was declared officially dead on December 8, the Solemnity of the Immaculate Conception. Latin-rite Christmas Day saw the Soviet flag lowered over Russia for the last time.

If God could do this, why couldn't he just change me! Surely I was a lot easier than the Soviet Empire. This was probably true, but the walls around my heart were just about as impenetrable as the one that used to divide Berlin.

Of course, he was already working.

Near the Basilica is also Fatima's own *via dolorosa*, Latin for *sorrowful way* or *journey*, also popularly known as the Stations of the Cross. These devotional shrines are common in the Catholic world, wherein the believer symbolically walks in the footsteps of Christ through a loosely-styled replica of the same path Jesus walked on the way to his crucifixion.

In a place like Fatima, so intimately connected with the Mother of God, it is no surprise that the town would have its own version of these devotions, right in the middle of town, almost like a city park. Much of Portugal is like that.

For example, later on in the pilgrimage, we were fortunate to visit the *Bom Jesus do Monte* (Good Jesus of the Mountain) Shrine, a five-star resort nestled in the mountains of northern Portugal near Braga.

Similarly, the Solemnity of the Assumption of the Blessed Virgin Mary is celebrated like the Fourth of July, complete with fireworks.

However, the park which houses the Stations of the Cross in Fatima is much simpler. This particular shrine, as I recall, is very natural. Much of the land is left the way it might have looked in 1917, with vegetation and trees still very much intact. There are even some holm oaks, the type of tree on which Our Lady is said to have stood during the apparitions. Along the path are miniature chapels containing each of the stations.

Upon our arrival, I could immediately tell that something strange was happening inside of me. The only way I can describe it is that there was this huge storm within; I felt as if I were being tossed to and fro on huge waves in this gargantuan dark ocean. I have never felt so alone in all my life. I felt . . . abandoned . . . empty.

The distress and agony of this time was so great that I thought I might physically fall over at times. It was so indescribably strange, and I still remember it, so many years later. The closest thing I could compare it to is an anxiety attack without any physical symptoms. There seemed to be this spiritual weight on my soul which grew heavier and heavier. I felt as if it could almost pull me down to the ground. It was an effort just to stand, let alone walk.

Finally, somewhere around the seventh station, the one which commemorates the second of Christ's three symbolic falls under the cross, I, too, fell to my knees and cried to heaven. As I prayed, I had the distinct sense, despite the serenity of my surroundings, that these hallowed grounds had really become a spiritual battleground and *I* was the disputed territory. I somehow knew that the celestial armies were battling those of the other kingdom over my immortal soul. I immediately thought of the final battle as depicted in the Book of Revelation:

A great portent appeared in heaven: a woman clothed with the sun, with the moon under her feet, and on her head a crown of twelve stars. . . . And another portent appeared in heaven: a great red dragon, with seven heads and ten horns, and seven diadems on his heads. . . . And the dragon stood before the woman who was about to bear a child, that he might devour her child when she brought it forth; she brought forth a male child, one who is to rule all the nations with a rod of iron. But her child was caught up to God and to his throne. . . . Then the dragon was angry with the woman and went off to make war on the rest of her offspring, on those who keep the commandments of God and bear testimony to Jesus. (Rv 12:1, 3–5, 17)

I would later realize that before that moment the devil had me right where he wanted me. I had believed many of his lies and thus had given him a lot of power over me. The Lord God of Hosts had decided it was time to take that ground back. The dark prince's power over me was about to end and he was not happy about it. I, for my part, could do nothing. I mean, I just stood there in my numbness as the mightiest armies in all the universe engaged in a cosmic battle around me.

In my powerlessness, I cried out to the Virgin of Fatima once more from the anguished depths of my being. "Blessed Mother," I prayed, "Help me! Do whatever you need to do to help me, but I cannot offer you anything; I am completely empty, drained, tired, and falling under the weight of this cross."

I would love to say that tears came but there were none. My heart was as dry as the dusty ground I was kneeling on. But then, somehow, I did it. I uttered the prayer which brought me to where I am today. It was a prayer that I had uttered many times before but never with such emptiness— it was the death gasp of my old self.

Yet, with that little tiny bit of spiritual strength, I did what many Christian faithful have done with Our Lady throughout the ages.

I bargained with this Jewish mother . . . sort of.

I made a vow to her which has resulted, ultimately, in this book now in your hands by saying, "If you show me the way and heal me, once I am restored, I will go back and bring others with me to the freedom you give me."

That was it, my last desperate plea. As it would turn out, that was all I needed to do. God's grace did the rest.

Somehow, I found it within me to get up and continue the Way of the Cross. The turmoil stayed with me until the end. Traditionally, the Way of the Cross has fourteen stations, starting with Jesus being sentenced to death and ending with his burial.

In recent times, some have added a fifteenth station focusing on Christ's resurrection from the dead. Upon my reaching this station, all the turmoil I felt all afternoon ceased immediately.

Heaven had spoken.

As she has done for over two millennia, the glorious "Woman Clothed with the Sun" had beaten the great red dragon.

Again.

Through the strength this great Woman imparted, I somehow did it. I knew I had just left my old self nailed there on the cross in the middle of Fatima.

I never took it back again.

"What Afflicted You Is Nothing"

"Listen, put it into your heart, my youngest son, that what frightened you, what afflicted you is nothing; do not let it disturb your face, your heart," the Blessed Virgin Mary said to St. Juan Diego on December 12, 1531.[17]

Although my encounter with the Mother of God happened under her title of Our Lady of Fatima, the words that begin this chapter are from an apparition in colonial Mexico which took place nearly five hundred years ago. Appearing there under the title of Our Lady of Guadalupe, she came as a pregnant Aztec princess with the same message of hope that she would bring to Portugal almost four centuries later.

She also left the Church of Mexico with a miraculous image on Juan Diego's *tilma* or cloak. Even today, the origin of the image on the *tilma* remains a fascinating and unexplained scientific mystery not unlike the Miracle of the Sun at Fatima or the Holy Shroud of Turin.

So, no matter what her title or the time and place, this great Woman Clothed with the Sun has come through time and space to the "rest of her offspring" upon whom the great dragon wages war. In my conversations with men who deal with SSA, I have come to believe that she has a special and

---

[17]   Carl Anderson and Eduardo Chavez, *Our Lady of Guadalupe: Mother of the Civilization of Love* (New York, NY: Doubleday, 2009), 15.

tender love for men like us, and I believe that if we seek her patronage, she will not rest until we are all safe in the hands of her divine Son.

That great battle that I experienced at the Way of the Cross was this great Woman acting on my behalf, making her claim over me and taking me from the dragon forever.

I still felt depressed, but as I got to know my fellow pilgrims, I began to realize that we were all on a journey. Therein lies the difference between a vacation and a pilgrimage. On a vacation, the primary goal is relaxation; on a pilgrimage, it is closer union with Jesus Christ and serves as a symbol of our lifelong Christian journey. Truly I began to see that we are all in this together and everyone has his or her own cross to bear. Traveling eight thousand miles from home merely served to remind me that this earth is not our true home and that we are all foreigners outside our true homeland who are destined for greater things.

My fellow pilgrims all carried their own burdens; for some, it was physical illness; for others, broken families or relationships; for still others, it was addiction or mental illness. For some, it was even a burden that someone in their own family was walking down the wrong path and the pilgrim had come to Fatima to offer prayers and sacrifices in union with Christ on his or her behalf.

The pilgrims on this particular journey were of various ages, but one thing that was quite unique was the number of young people, then the so-called Generation X. Due to the aforementioned "contest," there were roughly about two dozen people under the age of thirty. Being with young, believing Catholics was something totally new to me.

Growing up in a parish that was mostly comprised of older people, I had never been really exposed to young people at church. Most of the families who attended church with me were families who had worshiped there for generations as mine had. Many did not even reside in the inner-city neighborhood in which the church is situated.

For the first time, at Fatima I started to see those of my own generation struggling to live their faith in Jesus Christ against what were sometimes enormous obstacles.

In this world which, almost daily, becomes more and more hostile toward the sacred, many of my fellow pilgrims shared their stories—stories of sex, drugs, pornography, and general brokenness and lack of love in their lives. As I heard their testimonies, coupled with the magnificent faith of the people of Portugal, I began to see a framework rising from the ashes. I no longer felt alone, at least not as alone as before, but I was still lonely, locked in my self-imposed, solitary confinement.

Amidst everyone's struggles, although some paths were somewhat similar to mine, I still did not find hope for myself. I felt like Dorothy Gale in *The Wizard of Oz* when she realizes that the wizard has nothing in his bag for her. I felt certain that God was going to heal the addictions and some of the illnesses of my fellow pilgrims, but my homosexuality was something that I considered to be too ingrained in me to change. Would God really tamper with what I believed were my genetics? Would he really change who I thought I was? I thought not. Perhaps my prayers had once again gone unheard.

Perhaps, but maybe not.

Something was clearly happening, but I still wasn't sure what.

During Mass, the presence and power of the Lord Jesus Christ was unmistakable. At times, the Holy Spirit was so palpable! It reminded me, on a smaller scale, of what I had experienced the first time I attended a charismatic "healing" Mass. When our pastor had prayed over me, I felt a wave of love and warmth wash over me. I began weeping as I "rested" in the Spirit.

Attending Mass in Portugal was a little touch of that all over again. Our chaplains echoed what I had always heard and known but had somehow never taken into myself. All the time, they spoke about the need to invite Jesus into our hearts and accept him as our personal Lord and Savior. He needed to be the very center of our lives, they would preach, and nothing should ever come between us and him.

All that was necessary to experience Christ in our lives, they said, was to constantly ask him to enter and bring healing to our hearts. They also said that we needed to be open to the movement of the Holy Spirit in our lives. We needed to ask him to release his power and his gifts we had been given in baptism and only then would Christ be ready to use us to bring forth his kingdom.

Finally, a few nights before the end of the pilgrimage, I was moved so much that I decided to go to confession and confess what I had already confessed dozens of times, my abiding anger at the Lord and the events that fanned the flames of it in my heart.

I stood up in the aisle of the Latin Rite Chapel of the *Domus Pacis* hotel and waited for my turn in line. As the line dwindled, my anxiety and nervousness grew. This would only be the second time I had revealed my own struggles, again to a priest.

Finally, the confession line opened up and it was my turn. To my relief, the priest was behind the screen, not face-to-face. I say I was relieved because I really didn't know what to expect; I mean, I had heard horror stories about what some priests allegedly said in the confessional and I had only told one other living soul and that was a priest whom I knew and in whom I really trusted. I didn't know this guy at all.

Anyway, I swallowed the lump in my throat and began my confession, which consisted of more or less "normal" sins. Then, I let him have it, or so I thought.

"I have one more sin I need to confess," I said.

"Go ahead," he said gently in an Irish brogue.

"Well," I continued, "I want to confess the sin of anger—anger at God. I have confessed it over and over again, but I just can't shake it."

"Why are you angry at God?" he asked.

I stammered, "Well, this is kind of hard for me to say."

"Go on," he gently encouraged.

I summoned my remaining strength and blurted out, "I'm angry with God because I am gay and I don't understand how God could make me this way and then forbid me to express myself in the way that I am oriented."

Silence from behind the screen.

I had surely done it now; I must have shattered this poor priest's faith.

But then he asked me a question, "How do you know that God *made* you that way?"

That was an easy one.

"I am this way and I didn't choose to be and I've been this way as long as I can remember, so God must have made me this way," I explained.

Again, silence from behind the screen. Didn't have an answer for that one, did he?

He did—a simple one-word answer.

"No," he said.

"God *did not* do this to you," he said authoritatively and unequivocally. "People blame God all the time for things he doesn't do."

Although my mind had not yet arrived, my heart knew that what this priest was saying was true, but my mind kicked right in. At this point, my homosexuality seemed so permanent and immutable that it certainly seemed to me to have been part of who I was. How could it be anything but part of my very being? After all, that's what all the psychologists said. What else could this priest possibly tell me?

At that moment, I realized now how very weak and superficial my faith really was. I believed more in science than I did in the power of my Risen Lord. This priest helped me to begin to see this. He actually had an answer for me; I had heard part of what he said before, but somehow, coming from this priest, it seemed to have so much more authority.

So I asked, "If God didn't do this, then how did I get to be this way?"

"There could be a lot of reasons," he explained. "It could have something to do with the way you were brought up or there may have been some abuse in your past. I don't know you, so I really don't know specifically how or why you developed the way you did, but I know this: God *did not* make you that way, and he wants to heal you."

Heal me? *Healing is for people in wheelchairs, not for gay people*, I thought.

But I was intrigued.

"What do you mean?" I asked. "Are you telling me that I can *change* this?"

"Of course it can be changed!" he said emphatically.

"How?" I asked, puzzled to my core.

He repeated firmly, "You need to be healed."

Was he suggesting faith healing, like the Protestants do? What the psychologists say doesn't work? Was I going to be walking around with snakes next?

Yet, I persisted, "I just don't see how that's possible."

He responded, "*Then you don't know the power of Jesus Christ.* You need to bring this before him and you will be healed. The Lord will show you the way."

I was speechless. Was he kidding? Did he really think God would do this for me? Apparently, he did.

I stammered out my next words, "But what about my anger. I can't get rid of it."

"Don't worry about that. God is going to heal that *tonight*," he assured me.

Tonight? God was going to heal years of anger in an instant? Before I even had time to say anything else, he began invoking the name of the Lord Jesus and praying over me, asking God to heal me. Then, he gave me the required absolution from my sins.

"Through the ministry of his Church, may God grant you pardon and peace."

I began to feel strange.

"I absolve you from your sins."

It was a certain lightness of being.

"In the name of the Father, and of the Son, and of the Holy Spirit . . ."

Something had changed inside me.

". . . I absolve you from your sins. Go in peace and sin no more."

Peace.

Yes, that was the strange feeling.

Peace. *Shalom.* Peace—a feeling I had not known in many years.

Peace. The Peace of Jesus Christ.

The *Shalom* of the Messianic King.

At some point in my euphoria, I must have walked out of the confessional. That was it, just like that, I felt as if a burden had been lifted. My heart felt so free that it seemed I could soar with the eagles. My limbs felt like helium balloons. It was actually a physical sensation. To anyone watching, I must have looked drunk.

I was so afraid that I might start levitating that I hurried back to my pew and held on for fear that I would float away! A definite healing had occurred, that much I knew, but this was simply the first sign along the way of what would be a long, painful, and sometimes lonely journey into finding out who I truly was and what the Father really made me to be.

"Am I Not Here, I Who Have the Honor to Be Your Mother?"

After confessions were finished, I was so intrigued that I decided to find and "out" myself to the priest outside the seal of the confessional. I hoped that he could guide me in the right direction, toward this healing of which he spoke. I caught up with him as we left the hotel in the balmy night, with the basilica's illuminated white tower gleaming in the distance. I proceeded to introduce myself and identified myself through my confession. I thought there might be a feeling of awkwardness, but he either didn't feel awkward or, if he did, he didn't let it show.

I told him of my experience and how much the confession had meant to me and then asked him for additional guidance. This was all new to me, so I really had no idea what my next move should be. He smiled and said that he would help me out any way he could and that the primary thing I needed to do (in a nutshell) was to get in touch with my own masculinity, which, as he explained it, had somehow been lost in my sexual development, where I had not gotten what I needed as far as my own masculine identity.

Practically, this first meant seriously paying attention to my own prayer life and specifically asking Jesus to enter into my heart and heal it. Although I was still a bit skeptical that Jesus actually could *do* this, I now had in my heart a small glimmer of hope, which, like peace, was something I had not experienced in a very long time.

So I continued the remaining days of the pilgrimage renewed, but still feeling very alone in my struggle. Throughout the pilgrimage, I had come to befriend a man who I will call Mike. He was a few years my senior and served as a youth minister who also had the trip provided for him in the "contest." He was traveling with his fiancée, and during the trip, we really connected. We shared a lot about our lives and created a bond of friendship. We were together so often that people even called us by each other's name.

One night, Mike announced that he was going to keep vigil in the *capelinha* (pronounced kap-a-lean-ya), the little chapel which marks the original site of the apparitions, in order to pray for his upcoming marriage and his future bride. I decided that this was a really good idea and that I would also keep vigil on another night in this chapel of the apparitions as well. I would spend this night in prayer for healing and direction.

When facing the original basilica, the *capelinha* occupies the left side of the plaza, outside of the original basilica. It is basically a small, white, open-air sanctuary with a roof, which is built to protect the original "little chapel" that the Virgin had requested. In the center, there is an altar on which to celebrate Mass. To the right of the altar is a pillar of marble which encloses the tree stump from the holm oak on which Our Lady is said to have appeared. Said tree, unfortunately, died shortly after the apparitions due to overly enthusiastic pilgrims eager to have a piece of the very place where Our Lady stood.

On top of this pillar stands a statue of the Virgin designed according to how the visionaries described her.

It was on the Feast of Our Lady of Fatima, May 13, 1981 that his would-be assassin, Mohammed Ali Agca, snuck into Saint Peter's Square and shot the Holy Father at point blank range as he was greeting the crowds. Agca had perfect aim and should have killed the pope with a direct shot to the heart.

John Paul II publicly credited this "white Madonna" for interceding to save his life. Once he had recovered from his near-fatal wound, John Paul II made his own pilgrimage to Fatima in 1982 to formally give thanks to God and render homage to his Blessed Mother.[18]

With him, he brought the bullet the surgeons had extracted, and during a solemn liturgy with hundreds of thousands of fellow pilgrims, he permanently enshrined the bullet in the statue's crown as a testimony to the graces he obtained from Christ at the hands of his Mother.

In a strange twist of Divine Providence, for some reason, the jewel that was supposed to be in the center of the crown had never been placed when the crown was fixed upon the statue decades before John Paul's papacy. To everyone's surprise, the bullet brought by John Paul II fit the space *exactly*, as if the crown had been made to hold it![19]

---

[18]   Jason Evert, *Saint John Paul the Great: His Five Loves* (Lakewood, CO: Totus Tuus Press, 2014), 154.

[19]   Ibid., 152.

So it was in that little chapel, with the bullet from the side of Saint John Paul the Great and the tree on which Our Lady stood, that I kept my vigil. I prayed that, like the pope's doctors, Our Lady could perform her own surgery on me. I think that night was the longest time I have ever spent in continuous prayer, even to this day.

The evening was still and clear and there was a slight chill in the air. The votive candles behind the chapel flickered and pierced the darkness. I prayed the Rosary, dozed off, prayed in my own words, dozed off, read the Bible and dozed off again pretty much interchangeably throughout the night. Sometime in the wee hours of the morning, I was awakened by a group of German pilgrims, who, while I was dozing, had moved in and proceeded to celebrate Mass at four or five in the morning.

Since I felt kind of awkward sitting there curled up in my blanket, I decided to get up and participate in the Mass. I know not a word of German, yet I felt strangely at home among these people whom I did not know and whose language I could not comprehend. I still knew all the Mass parts and where I should respond, so I just responded and prayed in English.

It is at times like these that I feel humbled and blessed that God has called me to be part of the Universal Church, which knows no ethnic separation. Here I was in the middle of all these Germans, yet I worshipped with them and partook of the Lord's Body and Blood with them. I experienced true communion, without ever exchanging words with anyone.

This same Church awaited me back home.

But as great as these "mountaintop" experiences were, as the pilgrimage drew to a close, I became more and more keenly aware that I would soon return home to the United States and that this strength I had found here on pilgrimage might not accompany me home. I began praying about this concern with a sense of sadness and a twinge of fear creeping into my soul.

Fatima was my safe refuge; how would I go back?

Our Lady had an answer waiting for me.

It was the same answer she gave to St. Juan Diego in Guadalupe so many centuries before, "Am I not here, I who have the honor to be your Mother? Are you not in my shadow and under my protection? Am I not the source of your joy? Are you not in the hollow of my mantle, in the crossing of my arms? Do you need something more?"[20]

Was she not there who is my mother? Was I not under her shadow and protection? Was I not in the crossing of her arms?

Yes. She was indeed there, just as she has always been, and her Divine Son was about to change the course of my life forever.

---

[20]   Carl Anderson and Eduardo Chavez, *Our Lady of Guadalupe: Mother of the Civilization of Love* (New York, NY: Doubleday, 2009), 16.

"The Lord Whom You Seek Will Suddenly Come to His Temple"

One of my favorite Scriptures is the following one from the book of the prophet Malachi: "Behold, I send my messenger to prepare the way before me, and the Lord whom you seek will suddenly come to his temple; the messenger of the covenant in whom you delight, behold, he is coming, says the Lord of hosts. But who can endure the day of his coming, and who can stand when he appears?" (Mal 3:1–2).

It is, of course, a historical reference to the coming of the Divine Messiah entering the Holy Temple of Jerusalem in order to purify it and is often used in the liturgies of Advent and Lent. It reminds me of how suddenly the Lord can move in our lives. Sometimes we pray for years and years and the Lord seems so very far away, and then in one instant, he suddenly shows up.

That's what happened to me in Fatima.

A few days before my time there ended, Our Lady introduced me to the Man I had always been looking for.

The funny thing is that he had been there my whole life; I just never knew how much he loved me. He was the Lover who sought his beloved, but his beloved (me) didn't know he cared that much. Drawing heavily from the *Theology of the*

101

Body of his predecessor, Pope Benedict XVI explains this so beautifully in his inaugural encyclical *Deus Caritas Est* (*God Is Love*):

> The one God . . . loves with a personal love. His love, moreover, is an elective love: among all the nations he chooses Israel and loves her—but he does so precisely with a view to healing the whole human race. God loves, and his love may certainly be called *eros*, yet it is also totally *agape*. . . .
>
> . . . This is not only because it is bestowed in a completely gratuitous manner, without any previous merit, but also because it is love which forgives. . . .
>
> . . . [I]n Jesus Christ, it is God himself who goes in search of the "stray sheep", a suffering and lost humanity. . . . His death on the Cross is the culmination of that turning of God against himself in which he gives himself in order to raise man up and save him. This is love in its most radical form.[21]

Prior to my Fatima pilgrimage, I always knew that God existed; I was angry with him, but I never really doubted his existence.

However, believing that God exists is one thing, as St. James states, "You believe that God is one; you do well. Even the demons believe—and shudder" (Jas 2:19).

---

21   Benedict XVI, *Deus Carits Est,* December 25, 2005, nos. 9, 10, 12, http://w2.vatican.va/content/benedict-xvi/en/encyclicals/docu ments/hf_ben-xvi_enc_20051225_deus-caritas-est.html.

In other words, what good is it to simply believe in God if our actions don't bring forth good fruit from that faith? I had never fully realized the depth to which God knew *me* and loved *me*. That was the big difference. God knew me intimately and personally, but I was too wrapped up in myself to realize just how much he loved me: so much so that he took me away from all that was familiar to a strange land across the ocean to show me.

In this sleepy little Portuguese hamlet, the Lord of the Universe revealed himself to me personally. I learned beyond a shadow of a doubt that there is a God and that he knows me and loves me passionately. It surpassed all my previous understanding.

I struggled with coming to terms with my homosexuality for seven years.

During that time, I prayed, I cried, I prayed some more, I confessed, and I attended Mass. But instead of drawing closer to God, it seemed as if I were drifting further and further away from him. In just one night, that all changed and I finally realized that I already knew the One Man who could fill that emptiness and loneliness in my heart.

During those seven years of struggles, my prayers basically fell into a few distinct categories.

First, I prayed to meet another man who would truly know what was inside of me and understand my struggles.

I also prayed that I could believe in God again and that he would let me know in a tangible way that he existed and that he even cared about my life and what I did.

Next, I prayed and longed for a best friend that I never really had, a man who would love me for who I was, despite my struggles and my failings, someone I could hang out with and just do things with and feel like "one of the guys."

Finally, although I didn't really believe he necessarily could or would do it, I asked him to change my homosexual desires.

The first two of these prayers were answered that night. The third would be answered a few months later, and the last would be started but not fulfilled in a tangible way until many years later.

It started as my fellow pilgrim Mike and I discussed our lives together. We had been speaking for a number of hours. During that time, he had shared a number of his anxieties and vulnerabilities with me. Through these conversations, I think I discovered for the first time that this is really the basis for true intimacy. As Christians, we need to be able to make ourselves vulnerable before a trusted other, and that vulnerability is what leads to true sharing of lives in the bonds of fellowship. This is the great gift that Mike gave me that night.

This is what true love is and this is what I discovered I had been lacking since I made "the discovery" in adolescence and swore that no one would ever know my secret. I have always been a man of my word, even when my word might not have benefitted me. I closed in on myself rather than let my dirty little secret out.

I never loved, never really truly loved, never trusted another with my own pain. If that was my relationship to people, how could my relationship with God be any different? I had built that symbolic wall of Berlin around my heart, and as Our Lady of Fatima did to the wall in Germany, she was about to knock down this one as well. I came to realize that there was only one way this could happen.

I felt called to share this with Mike.

Of course, I had shared with priests before but that was different. Catholics have this thing called the "seal" of confession. It means that the priest is forbidden under pain of excommunication from revealing the sins of the penitent to anyone for any reason. The priest must take that knowledge to the grave, even at personal risk to himself.

I now had to take the chance and trust another human being *without* the seal of confession.

Now, deciding to share my struggle with Mike was not a spur of the moment decision, nor was it something I took lightly. I had begun considering it as soon as our friendship began to grow. I finally decided that if I didn't do it now, there might not be another opportunity. We lived states away from each other, so I knew that even if it didn't go well, I never had to see him again.

I *needed* to take this risk.

And so it was. I decided to take what was, unbeknownst to me, my first big step toward healing my homosexuality.

This was probably the hardest time I ever had telling anyone. My stomach was in knots and I was shaking like a leaf.

Seeing how upset I was, Mike said, "You know, you don't have to tell me if you don't want to."

"No," I said. "It is time."

I summoned up all the strength I had. What would he think? Would he be repulsed? Would he run from the chapel screaming? The time had come. I had to find out.

"Mike," I stammered. "I, Uh, I, I'm . . . *gay*."

There. I had done it.

I dropped the H-Bomb on him, too, and he didn't have the armor of a Roman collar and a purple stole to withstand it.

His response was one I had not expected.

"Why do you say that?" he asked.

Was he kidding? Did he really want me to explain how a guy comes to know he's gay? Did he need this spelled out?

He wasn't going to make this any easier, so I answered him literally, "I'm sexually attracted to men, Mike."

"Well, I gathered *that*!" he said. "What I mean is why are you labeling yourself as 'gay'?"

"Because that's who I am," I said.

"So you think that because you're attracted to men that you are automatically identified as gay?" he asked.

"Well . . . yeah," I responded.

Wasn't that how it usually worked? Men who are sexually attracted to women are straight, men who like men are gay. It seemed simple to me.

The truth, I found, was actually a lot more complex than that. This would be the first in a long line of misconceptions that the Lord Jesus would be correcting in me over many years.

"No," Mike said. "You're thinking about this in the wrong way. What you have are attractions to the same sex. What you need to decide is if these attractions define who you are. Is that who you are?"

I was really mystified now. Wasn't it?

I thought it was; I didn't like it, but I thought it was.

All at once, I caught a glimpse of a new world of possibilities, a new way of viewing my life and my identity. It was thrilling and terrifying at the same time. Could it be that I was not to be forced to carry this burden, or maybe that it could at least be a little lighter?

I answered Mike honestly, "I don't know. I mean, I don't want it to be, but what else is there?"

"Freedom," he answered, "and healing."

There was that word again.

Healing.

The same word from confession.

Healing.

"What do you mean . . . *healing*?" I asked, really bewildered now.

"I mean that you can be free of homosexuality, but when you say you're gay, that language indicates that you have surrendered to that identity. Is that what you want?" he asked me.

"No. Of course not. It has never been what I wanted," I said, remembering all the tears and the pain that this had caused me through the years. "Of course I don't want it," I repeated, "but how can you tell me to just change it. It doesn't feel like something that I have the power to change. You don't know what it's like to be gay."

What he said next would change my life forever.

Mike looked me square in the eyes and asked pointedly, "How do you know?"

Now, this was just too much. This man who was about to be married couldn't be insinuating what I thought he was insinuating.

I continued, "Well, I don't know, but I am just assuming . . . I mean, you're getting married, aren't you?"

He looked at me and smiled as he related his own story of overcoming same-sex attraction to the point that he was now ready for marriage. I asked him how this was possible, and he told me that it took plenty of discipline, prayer, and years of healing. He said that it was a very painful journey but one that was worth it.

So this was *possible*, I thought.

Wow.

I almost couldn't wrap my mind around it.

It was too much.

All of the sudden, I had a keen sense of the Blessed Mother; in the eyes of my heart, I could see her smiling, and with the ears of my heart, I heard her saying to me interiorly, "See, God has heard and answered all your prayers; come and meet my Beloved Son again and let him heal you."

Another *kiss* from Our Lady.

This was the moment in my life when I came to realize that God was *truly real*. There was no doubt about it. He is not a figment of my (or anyone's) imagination but a real and powerful Being who knew me and loved me personally and listened to my every word, even though he sometimes seemed so far away.

After seven years of slavery, anger, and self-hatred, I was again enraptured in his love and this love brought me freedom. The seventh year—the biblical year of freedom decreed in the Torah, during which all the slaves were to be set free, "When you buy a Hebrew slave, he shall serve six years, and in the seventh he shall go out free, for nothing" (Ex 21:2).

Our Great Lord had once again brought liberty to his captive son. I could almost feel the exultation of the Blessed Virgin and the saints and angels as they reunited this lost son with his loving Father once again.

I was loved.

He heard me after all.

August Mother that she is, Our Lady never let me fall until she was sure that I could fall nowhere but into the strong, loving arms of her Risen Son.

In bringing me to her great basilica, Our Lady had procured for me the answer to all my prayers. I had a new mission and a new life was just beginning for me. God had restored my faith and hope through the love of the Blessed Virgin and the friend I had longed and prayed for.

As in the Book of Malachi, the Lord entered the temple of my soul suddenly and unexpectedly that night. Right there in that chapel, I gave my whole heart to Jesus Christ and promised that I would do that which Our Lady commanded the head waiter of Cana in the Gospel of John (2:5) to do.

"Do whatever he tells you."

I knew also that he would eventually bring with him the pain of the Refiner's Fire to purify me.

I was ready.

Mike and I talked for hours into the dawn. As the sun rose over the great basilica the next morning, I would begin a new, exciting, and sometimes painful journey toward wholeness and healing. When I came to Fatima, I was a boy; when I left, I started to understand how to become a man.

This "kiss" from Our Lady was different from all the others, for with it, she was sending me on a new journey into the world of men, with her Divine Son by my side—the only man who could ever truly fill that hole in my heart.

Adeus, Fatima!

"See What Love the Father Has Given Us"

When I left the "Land of Holy Mary," I still had some trepidation as to what would happen when I returned, but these fears largely melted away as I basked in the love of God. Anyone who has experienced an encounter with Jesus Christ knows what I'm talking about. I felt like I was king of the world, indestructible and answerable only to One. All the colors seemed brighter and all sensations more profound. I felt so free that at times, I would actually lift my hands into the air in a triumphant *V*.

People around me noticed too.

I remember my father (who never knew about my struggles) saying, "I don't know what happened over there, but whatever it was, it sure was good. You're a different person."

Indeed, I was a different person.

Despite all this, I have to say that immediately after Fatima, nothing really changed for me as far as my struggles with homosexuality. The same desires that had always been there still were; the difference was that I now knew that Jesus Christ was by my side and I needed fear nothing.

It would be years before I'd been healed enough to say something like I said at the beginning of this book, "I *used* to be gay."

Change and healing rarely come overnight. I was no exception. I think that in my previous, more childish relationship with God, I expected that when I prayed, he would wave his magic wand over and, *poof*, I'd be healed, that I could just "pray the gay away."

That may happen for some people sometimes, but that's not often the way the Lord works with me. Usually, there is some defining moment where God pours out his grace in a concrete way, which kind of kick-starts the process, and then Christ and the believer work things out together, very gradually.

God seems to operate this way, at least for some, for a couple of reasons.

First, with issues like homosexuality, where a person's identity is so central to the problem, God is not usually going to just take the identity away, even though it might be a maladaptive one. As I began to conquer my same-sex attractions, I remember the fear I had in totally redefining myself; it is not a comfortable place to be.

It was much easier for me to lust after men than to try to find out how my heart was broken and then ask the Father to heal it. It seems like a paradox, but for men like me, hiding behind same-sex attraction really is easier than working on the pain within us.

So God, in his mercy, healed me gradually, not instantaneously.

Thus, one important aspect of this kind of sexual healing is a consistent prayer life. For Catholics, this means frequent participation in the sacraments. It was Mike who taught me this truth. He told me that it was one of the primary steps I needed to take toward healing. He told me that it was not enough to simply go to Mass on Sunday; I needed to go every day whenever possible and implore the Lord constantly to reveal me to myself and bring all the dark and painful parts into the light.

I did what Mike said. I went to Mass every day, sometimes in different churches. Wherever I attended Mass, invariably all the old ladies always told me that they thought I should be a priest.

While I was honored, I have to say that I think it speaks poorly of the Catholic Church as a whole because, essentially, the underlying statement there is that young men do not attend daily Mass or pray unless they're thinking about the priesthood. This completely contradicts the teachings of the Second Vatican Council (*Lumen Gentium* 40, 41) which emphasized the *universal* call to holiness. The Council Fathers reemphasized the Church's teaching that holiness is not just the domain of ordained ministers and consecrated celibates.

Thus, here I was, trying to be holy by seeking the healing of my broken sexuality. However, Mass and the sacraments alone could only take me so far, despite their great efficacy, grace, and power. In the Gospels, Christ always talked about the need to experience his coming *in the flesh*. He himself came that way. He could have appeared glorious in the clouds as he will in his triumphant return at the end of time, but instead, he chose to take a human body from the flesh of a Virgin. "And the Word became flesh and dwelt among us, full of grace and truth; we have beheld his glory, glory as of the only Son from the Father" (Jn 1:14).

That might have been easy for those followers who walked the roads he walked with him or ate and drank with him, but more than two thousand years later, how is it possible for a believer to commune with Jesus in the flesh? It is true that he did leave us sacraments which are the visible signs of his grace. All these sacraments, particularly the sacrament of Reconciliation and the Blessed Sacrament of the Lord's Body and Blood, are essential for any kind of healing, particularly sexual healing.

I gradually came also to understand that I also needed Christ's Mystical Body on earth—that is, the Church—to experience healing. Specifically, I needed to know other men deeply and intimately in order to find that lost part of my own masculinity and find Jesus Christ, the True Man *in the flesh*.

This was to be my next very difficult and painful but deeply fulfilling part of my journey toward healing.

Mike had actually set me off on my journey of discovery into the world of masculinity that night in Fatima. It was he who told me that I needed to experience being with men and learning from other men. This left me at somewhat of a loss. I had no idea how I could do this.

After Fatima, Mike had sent me a book about healing homosexuality which I read as quickly as I could. I also did a web search on this new thing called the internet, which led me to many other books and websites that I read voraciously, trying to get to the root of my issues. All the books and web-sites concurred with what Mike had told me about the need to reconnect to the masculine world.

This was a problem. Many years of sinking into my own pain and my worlds of imagination had left me unable to function in peer groups, particularly with men. I was almost afraid to be with them for fear that they would then see how *unmanly* I really was. In life, people generally take the path of least resistance, yet here I was, forced to take the path of *most* resistance.

But that is the true way to growth and holiness. I myself wasn't even sure that this would actually work, but I knew at the deepest level of my being that homosexuality was not in God's plan for me and that I could not feel free while I was in its grip. And Jesus Christ, I knew, had called me to be free.

Besides Mike and, by that point, several priests, I had never really confided my "deep, dark secret" to anyone. It was really a terrifying process for me because I was still very much in the throes of my same-sex attractions. It was not yet a thing of the past and I really did not know how men would react.

But risk was the name of the game at this point, so after much prayer, I ended up confiding in select men whom I thought would be able to handle it.

Through and with these men, I totally immersed myself in the masculine world. I went on retreats, to prayer groups, social gatherings, concerts, and just about anywhere there was a group of guys that I could get to know.

Although I never actually made deeper connections with a lot of these men, over time, I began to view the male world differently. I actually focused on areas that I had avoided for years. I tried my hand at informal sports and observed male culture to see anew what it was that I had rejected so many years before. The lack of male influence in my own family and what I had experienced as a sensitive boy in school had hardened my feelings about men into an ambivalence. Some of that was now starting to change as I experienced interaction with different types of men, particularly spiritual men. Thus, the healing continued.

Before this, I had viewed my struggles with same-sex attraction as the obstacle to my holiness. Now, I was beginning to see that my sanctification was not occurring despite my same-sex attractions but *because of them and through them.*

SSA is my true cross that will lead to my salvation. I also begin to see that my struggle was also leading others to God and drawing them into an ever-deeper relationship with Jesus Christ. The Lord was using my struggle to sanctify the other members his Church.

These words began to take on personal meaning for me as I began to see the Lord *as actually present* in my struggles.

Learning to become part of Christ's Mystical Body anew did not just entail hanging out with and learning about men and their lives. I also began to build up my spiritual life, much the way an athlete builds his body in order to perform well. I kept up with regular fasting; I prayed, attended daily Mass, made confession frequently, and sought out opportunities for healing, including prayer groups, retreats, and "healing" Masses. I was prayed over, prayed for, and prayed about by a lot of people.

Prayer *always* works.

So it was one day when I arrived at one of these prayer groups that I met the man of my prayers. I met the man who would become the best friend that I had always longed for. Throughout my years of self-imposed exile, I had effectively shut myself off from human contact with few exceptions.

Josh walked into the prayer meeting one night. We made an instant connection, based primarily on the fact that we were both driving in from the same town. We decided to carpool together, and with a half-hour each way, there was a lot of time to get to know each other very well.

Josh had just recently returned home from a graduate program in another state where he had experienced a deep conversion which had ultimately led him out of the Catholic Church and into a sectarian denomination. He had recently left this community and returned to the Catholic Church. He came back to New Jersey upon the completion of his degree and had just begun a new job locally.

That was perfect for me. It is what I had always wanted, a good Catholic friend living close by. Our relationship deepened as we hung out and did things together. We prayed together a lot and just went out and did fun stuff all the time. We shared a lot of our struggles, trials, goals, and dreams. It was not uncommon (at the time, before marriage and kids) for us to converse for hours, whether in person or on the phone.

It was a time of great healing for me because I had always viewed myself as unaccepted and unacceptable by the male culture. Yet here was this very masculine man who wanted me as his friend. The Lord really knew what he was doing when he sent Josh into my life. He has all the characteristics that made him what I considered to be a "real man." Besides that, he was a man of faith and a man who I could tell loved me as much as I loved him. I just wasn't exactly sure why.

Josh is and always has been very secure in his masculinity. I remember the night I told him about my struggles. His reaction puzzled me.

He actually laughed out loud.

He didn't believe me.

"Really?" he asked, laughing. "I could never tell."

"Why are you laughing?" I asked, a little uncertain of the situation.

"I'm sorry," he said. "That's just an area I don't understand. I've always been really secure in that area of my life. I just don't get it, so I'm just not sure how to react, but one thing I can tell you is that it doesn't change our friendship. I love you as much as I ever did, and I'll support you through this any way I can."

That was all I needed to hear. The fear melted away as he gave me a big bear hug. We kept our friendship together over the next two decades, and although we had ups and downs, our loyalty toward each other had always remained. He gave me what I consider to be the greatest honor any man can give another when he asked me to be his best man and then the godfather of his firstborn son. He eventually moved to another state, but we still keep in contact and visit regularly. I would have the double honor of having him reciprocate as my best man and godfather of my first daughter years later.

He would also prepare me for my next step.

Through him and other men in my life, I learned to really value my male friends and the relationships that I had with them. They were honest, open, loving, and caring, yet somehow, I still did not feel satisfied. It was as if I could not get enough.

I still ached to be held and touched by men. As I continued to be healed of my same-sex attraction, fully experiencing the pain of this longing was the next step. As I moved away from sexual attraction, I was left with my raw and aching need for male affirmation that I never got growing up. The great majority of these longings were no longer erotic in nature, but I felt always driven to seek more and more, never seeming able to fill the void that I felt so profoundly.

One day, I was serving on a retreat team. After our holy hour, we offered to pray with anyone who wished. After we were finished, I went up to the guy who had served as my "prayer-partner" and hugged him in support and thanks for what had been a moment of grace for many people. Then, something unusual happened.

He did not let me go.

He pulled me against him. At first, it felt very awkward and I was a little scared. I don't think I ever had a man be so affectionate with me, especially not in public! I had to fight the urge to break free of his embrace.

But at the same time, *I liked it.*

It felt so good to be there in his arms, so safe and secure that I let myself relax and returned his embrace. I had never really experienced anything like this before.

For so many years, because of my SSA, I felt that the type of masculine affirmation I needed was just not there. I didn't think it existed. I thought I would have to be gay to experience a man's love that way. But suddenly, now there was no need to grasp at masculinity or lust after it because this man gave it to me to freely.

He shared his masculinity with me in a way that was chaste, good, and holy.

The emotions of it all overwhelmed me and I began to sob. He only held me tighter. The whole experience probably lasted no more than five minutes or so, but I wished it could have gone on forever.

Afterwards, I was so emotionally overwhelmed that I could barely think. I felt the presence of God in a tangible way that I had never known before. I was so overcome with the love of God and I had a great sense of joy and healing which lasted throughout the night.

Finally, I had physically shared in manhood and the Fatherhood of God was revealed to me in a most powerful way.

Later, this experience led me to seek other, similar experiences, and the next was through my good friend Isaac. We were in the same Masters Counseling program at Franciscan University and had worked on many projects together and as a result a friendship developed. I also got to know his wife and son (who would eventually be joined by six more children).

They were and are such a wonderful example of a good Christian family and I always enjoyed being with them. They demonstrated to me the sacrifices which are a part of marriage and family life.

Isaac also showed me how to properly treat a woman through the love and devotion which he expressed to his wife. It was not a sentimental and fluffy devotion but one that is real and solid.

Isaac had grown up with brothers and expressed to me how much he valued their love and affection and how much he missed that since they were so many miles away.

He made it OK *and even normal* for me to desire physical affection from men.

We began to share our lives and struggles in a very real and candid way. I told him of my struggles, and he was very affirming and supportive. I even told him about how uncomfortable I was with my body's own physical reaction to receiving affection from men.

He told me that he was perfectly comfortable with it and encouraged me to own the emotions I was feeling and to express them physically and appropriately. I had never felt like I had the permission to do that before.

So, before we parted company after our Thursday afternoon lunches, we would pray together and share a parting, long hug. It felt so good to be in his embrace. I felt so safe and so loved.

This unabashed male bond, whether expressed physically in manly embrace or not, is indeed the true essence of masculinity, and Isaac both exemplified and summed it up so well for me. Isaac was so real and down-to-earth. He brought the Fatherhood of God to me as only another man can.

I told him that I wished I had this growing up and how I'd always longed for an older brother like him.

He replied, "You have one now."

Through Isaac, I learned that as Christian men, we are all called to this mediation of the Fatherhood of God through our own masculinity. We are called to share our lives, our struggles, our very selves with our brothers. It is the way we experience Jesus in the flesh as noted in 1 John 3:1–3. "See what love the Father has given us, that we should be called children of God; and so we are. The reason why the world does not know us is that it did not know him. Beloved, we are God's children now; it does not yet appear what we shall be, but we know that when he appears we shall be like him, for we shall see him as he is. And every one who thus hopes in him purifies himself as he is pure."

This is indeed the love that the Father bestows which reveals who we truly are.

The Knights and Their Queen

I t was one thing to relate to men as individuals, like I did with Josh and Isaac, but I still somehow needed to get into the *world* of men. I now needed to learn how to relate with other men in groups.

For that, the Lord would send me away again to a (sometimes very) strange land, but as always, he sent his Mother ahead to prepare. As I graduated from college, I began to feel that he was calling me to discern graduate school, specifically to pursue a master's degree in counseling at a very unique school.

Largely overlooked by many, Franciscan University is located in the rust belt town of Steubenville, Ohio. It was and is renowned as one of the most dynamic and most faithful of all the Catholic universities in the United States, if not the world.

Largely through the work of the late Father Michael Scanlan, TOR, the university transformed from one of the nation's biggest "party schools" into a bastion of Catholic orthodoxy. One of the ways he accomplished this was through a system known as households which, by their nature, are open to either exclusively men or women.

At a risk of oversimplifying these complex and inspiring organizations, a men's household is almost a cross between a covenant community and a fraternity. It is a fraternity in the truest sense of the word because it is based entirely on brotherhood. The men pray together, have fellowship together, and love each other unconditionally. From the beginning, the household experience was powerful and intense.

I never had brothers growing up, but the bond we had and the love we all shared was like nothing I have experienced before or since. It was an incredible bond, even with brothers I didn't know that well or at all. It truly changed my life and made me the man I am today.

It was another of Our Lady's great "kisses" for me.

I still don't fully understand how I arrived on the campus of Franciscan University. The only thing I really knew about it was what I had seen on the *Eternal Word Television Network* (EWTN), and quite frankly, it didn't make a great impression on me. It seemed like a tiny little school out in the boondocks of Ohio.

Even when I said that name, people would mockingly say, "Stupid-ville?"

Apparently, as the Scriptures (1 Cor 1:25) say, the foolishness of God is so much wiser than men. As my last year of college rolled around, I was considering grad schools, and all of a sudden, the thought of Steubenville crossed my mind.

I quickly dismissed it thinking, "No, I want to go to a *real* school for graduate studies."

But the thought was persistent. Somehow, I knew that I was supposed to be there. God was *calling* me to be there.

Our Lady was waiting there for me.

I was convinced.

One of my journal entries from 1997 when I was still exploring the school reads:

> I got prayed over at a Festival of Praise [at Francis-
> can University of Steubenville] and one of the women
> praying over me said that I had been "very blessed by
> God" and Our Lady was forming me to be a "man
> of justice", a "true leader" and a "warrior". Another
> woman said that Our Lady would show me true man-
> hood and would continue what she began in Fatima.

As far as I recall, these folks would have no way of knowing what was going on inside me or even that I had been to
Fatima, much less what had happened there! So this was to
be yet another "land of Holy Mary" to which the Queen
Mother invited me to come, this time not on pilgrimage but
as a student. I would not leave for two weeks this time but
for two years.

Like the great column of cloud or the pillar of fire from
the Old Testament, the Blessed Virgin was showing yet
another way to a deeper relationship with Jesus Christ—the
next step on my journey, and it was a big one.

So, in August of 1998, I found myself in that dinky little
rust belt town that time seemed to have forgotten, looking
for a place to live and beginning the pursuit of my master's in counseling. I wasn't yet sure exactly what I was doing
there, but I knew that this was the next layer of my healing.

In my research about the university, I had already learned
about the household system and I knew that I was going to
join one. But which one? There were at least twenty when I
was there and I really didn't know what to expect.

The first place I started to look was at what is called a
Household Life Mass, which is a liturgy where the entire

household system comes together for worship. The first one of the school year would be held on August 28, the Feast of Saint Augustine of Hippo, outside under the trademark Summer Conference "big top" tent for which the university is famous.

Household representatives all processed in one at a time, holding up the banner of their respective household. As the music ministry played "Lift High the Banners of Love," I saw the banner of my future household, *The Knights of the Holy Queen*, and was instantly attracted to it.

Every household also prints its own unique t-shirt that all members were supposed to wear on designated "shirt" days, one of which is the Household Life Mass. The shirt of the Knights was a beige one with a stylized image of the Virgin Mary on the front and various quotations from the Scriptures and St. Maximilian Kolbe on the back, all in dark blue ink. I grew more and more intrigued with these men and I had to find them, so I positioned myself so I could see who they were. Once I saw them, I felt an inspiration in my heart.

It was as if Our Lady whispered to me in the deep recesses of my soul, "Go to these men, your brothers. This is where I have called you."

From that moment on, I had no doubt. This was where I was supposed to be.

She had told me.

As I began to join these men in their weekly prayers, that sense of belongingness grew and grew. We were from very different walks of life and had equally varied spirituality and lifestyles. There was a large contingent from the great city of

New Orleans, another from Southern California, and many other regions of the United States. Some of us were studious. Others not so much.

We used to say that there were only two things we had in common: the first was that we had *nothing* in common, and the second was that we knew we were specially chosen by Our Holy Queen to be together as a brotherhood.

One of the things that exemplifies for me the whole experience of how different we all were from each other is a Rosary made for me by one of my brothers. It is unique because it is woven of hemp fiber. It is, to me, a beautiful work of art and exemplifies the need that we all have to sanctify the goods of the world in the name of Jesus Christ.

When we are "knighted", all the knights take a "Sir" name of a saint to whom they have devotion or to whom they feel otherwise drawn, similar to the way consecrated religious take a new name when they enter a community.

In similar fashion to fraternities, we also had "big brothers" that more or less sponsored us as we discerned into household. We called our "big" our "model knight," while those of us who were not yet knighted were called "squires." The model knight's job is basically to instruct prospective knights in the ways of household. He is there to serve as an example of service and loyalty. This culminates in an initiation ceremony, which reinforces the idea that we are there to serve each other as Christ served us.

Later on in the semester, there is a knighting ceremony where all the new knights pledge their loyalty to each of the older knights and one another by embracing, looking each other straight in the eye, and stating, "Brother to brother, through life, death, and all eternity, in honor of Mary Our Queen and Jesus Our King."

I don't think I can put into words the profound effect all these rituals were having in my soul. God's grace was poured out on me through these men in a very tangible and concrete way, but not a way that I can clearly explain. I remember clearly the day I wore the household shirt for the first time.

When I put it on, I felt a physical stirring in my body. It was as if my own dormant manhood was rising up from within me. I felt as if I had found a piece of myself that had been lost, or at least hidden for a long time. I felt whole. For the first time in my life, I felt like a man. I had made it into the world of men. I was at last, "one of the guys."

I was a *Knight*.

The Knights of the Holy Queen is more than just a household. Every one of us believes that we were specifically and personally chosen by Our Lady to be a part of it. It's just bigger than any of us; all of us would testify to that.

Many of our brothers have gone on to do amazing things for the Church, the most publicly famous of whom are probably Chris Stefanick, the founder of *Real-Life Catholic*, and Chris Stewart of *Casting Nets Ministries*. Others may not have the same public notoriety but nonetheless serve the Church as priests, teachers, theologians, professors, and diocesan and parish staff. They also serve in Catholic schools and other organizations that further the mission of the Church in spreading the Gospel.

Most, however, live quieter and even *heroic* lives in the world as devoted husbands and fathers. I couldn't possibly be prouder of these great men. I am so incredibly blessed and humbled to count myself among them.

If I meet a brother that I have not seen in a number of years, when we finally meet again, it is like that time apart never existed. Intimacy is almost instantly re-established. I can't even say that I was super close to all of these men, yet I know in the deepest depths of my being that they are my brothers and always will be and that even if I never see some of them again on earth, our fellowship will reassemble in the kingdom.

Even now, many of us who went to school at the same time still keep in contact almost daily via an email group because we are scattered throughout not only the country but the world. Since so many of us are now busy with our primary vocations or just searching out the path God has set for our lives, our brotherhood has now become largely a "virtual" one, though no less real. We still share that great bond of serving the Queen of Heaven.

Our Lady keeps us all of us, her sons, together and spiritually close despite the distance.

Being a Knight is truly profound and still affects me deeply.

One night many years later, I had a dream about it. I was in a large, empty room alone and then, one by one, the Knights began to come into the room. Our greetings were very brief, and then each Knight would grab a drink and pull up a chair and start talking. More and more Knights kept coming in until finally the whole room was full. Everyone was talking and laughing and just enjoying being together.

It was one of those dreams that left an ache in my heart, that I wished had been true.

Then the Lord, in his goodness, made it true. About twelve years after I left Franciscan University, I had the opportunity to see a group of these guys again during a reunion in Florida. Knighthood was so incredible at Franciscan, and I wondered if it would still be so after all that time had passed.

The last time I saw some brothers, we were boys; now we were men. I wondered if things would be the same? Indeed, lots of things changed, but when I walked into the place we were staying, everyone greeted me not as if it had been twelve years but maybe twelve days. I couldn't believe how easily things picked up where we last left off.

A decade just vanished and who we are now just became a part of our fellowship. A lot of guys said it was like heaven, not in a paradise vacation sense of the word, but in a true sense of communion. It was truly a huge spiritual event, yet like God, so still and so peaceful.

If that weren't enough, we then had another reunion in New Orleans which was just as great as the first one. We again left feeling refreshed and renewed simply by being in each other's company. More reunions followed and they were all great.

I say it often and I mean it literally and without exaggeration; these guys made me the man I am.

We have all felt the hand of our most loving and powerful Queen on our backs. There is such a tenderness and depth of love among these men. I am proud to call them my brothers. Our covenant was not one limited only to our time at the university but one that we strive to live all of our lives.

I try to keep this covenant at the forefront of every day. To me, being one of Our Lady's Knights is not a boys' club that I joined back in college. I know that I am specially chosen by her as an instrument to bring the Gospel of Jesus Christ to the world and usher in the Triumph of her Immaculate Heart and that these men are there to help me do it as I am there to help them.

It is sometimes said that a man never really truly comes into his own until he is accepted into a group of other men who love, accept, and defend him unconditionally. He needs to feel that he belongs to his group, his clan, his *tribe*. Men *need* other men.

The positive manifestations of this need to belong include the many fraternal men's organizations in the Church. Conversely, in our fatherless society, the dark side of this is the proliferation of gangs and fraternities based largely on sin and selfishness instead of service and love. Nonetheless, both testify to the need men have to be with other men. This is obviously something that goes beyond those of us who struggle with same-sex attraction.

Although I have since joined (and even started) other men's groups, it is always because of the inspiration I got from these guys.

They are truly *my tribe*.

My pack.

My faternity.

My boys.

My brothers.

With their strength and power behind me, I know I can do anything, and as one or our household songs goes, "I will fear nothing."

"Totus Tuus, Maria!"

One night, I had a pretty intense dream. I was in a room with a bunch of women who were singing the praises of abortion on demand. As they became more and more vocal, I felt convicted to tell these women that they were killing human beings through their "choices."

Obviously, they did not like what I had to say, and they turned on me in the dream, screaming at me. As their levels of anger rose, I began to feel physically threatened. All of a sudden, from behind me, I felt Our Lady enter the room. I never saw her, but I felt her presence. She came up from behind me and dropped her mantle over me. As her mantle fell, I felt her embrace me from behind and I was enveloped in a sense of peace and joy as I fell back into her arms.

As I was falling backwards, she whispered in my ear, "God is very pleased with you."

Then, I woke up, and although I knew it was a dream, there was a real spiritual quality about it and that sense of peace stayed with me throughout the next day to the point that I would become so overcome with emotion during the day that I would just break down weeping.

I am not sure why I had this particular dream at this particular time in my life. I wasn't really involved in anything specifically having to do with the pro-life movement, but as I meditated on it further, I came to realize that I have always been under Our Lady's patronage. Indeed, the Mother of God has always taken me as her own and I knew that I would one day be at the forefront of the fight for the culture of life.

I remember attending prayer meetings where complete strangers would come up to me and tell me that they saw Our Lady with me or that they could feel her protection around me. I can affirm that this is true based on my own experiences in my life, at Fatima, even here in my dreams. There were just so many kisses from her throughout my life.

When I have shared my struggles with my sexuality with people and I tell them how deeply seated my desires were, they often ask, "Why didn't you ever succumb to them?"

The only answer I can offer is that I am under what I like to call the "Immaculate Protection." I owe it to none other than Jesus Christ with the special intercession of his Mother. It is no strength on my part at all; of that I am convinced.

So, since Our Lady seemed to have taken me for her own and placed me under her protection, it seemed only logical that I should formally offer myself to her. It was time to offer a kiss back to her. Not just a kiss, but my whole life, which she herself had ransomed for me in the name of Jesus Christ. Indeed, I would be nothing and nowhere without her. I say that without exaggeration.

I did this using what is commonly known as the "Total Consecration to Our Lady," or more simply, the "De Montfort Consecration," named after St. Louis de Montfort, the great priest who spread this devotion and wrote the "textbook" on it known as *True Devotion to Mary*.

I first formally did the total consecration on the feast of the Immaculate Conception when I was still a student at

Franciscan University. In many ways, it was probably the capstone of my time there and the most important thing I did, besides my Knighthood.

De Montfort advises that those seeking to make the consecration prepare for thirty-three days beforehand to properly dispose the soul to the grace of the moment and that the consecration be done on a major feast of Mary. I did the preparation with the men in my household during a college-wide consecration on the solemnity of the Immaculate Conception.

It was an unseasonably warm December evening and quite a sight as well over one thousand college students gathered in and around Christ the King Chapel, which could hold only two to three hundred people at most. Thus, there was an overflow crowd of hundreds of college students waiting outside as we all made our consecration together. I will never forget kneeling there on the concrete sidewalk with my household brothers as we all offered ourselves to Our Lady as one.

Saint John Paul II used the phrase "Totus Tuus" as his papal motto to indicate his devotion to the Virgin Mary. This comes directly from the teaching of St. Louis de Montfort and means "Totally Yours." The complete formula reads, "Totus tuus ego sum, et omnia mea tua sunt. Accipio te in mea omnia. Praebe mihi cor tuum, Maria."

I belong entirely to you, and all that I have is yours. I take you for my all. O Mary, give me your heart.[22]

---

[22]   Louis De Montfort, *True Devotion to Mary: With Preparation for Total Consecration* (Charlotte, NC: TAN Books, 2010), no. 233.

Some people shorten that to simply, "Totus tuus, Maria!" *I am all yours, Mary!*

In essence, what I and all those college students really did was to renew our baptismal vows to Jesus Christ through the Blessed Virgin. This entailed offering ourselves completely to the Mother of Jesus so that she can perfect the work of Christ in us and make our own works more efficacious.

Thus, we offered to her all our prayers, works, sufferings, hopes, and dreams and allow her to dispose of them as she wishes. In return, she covers the believer in her mantle and presents him or her to Christ through her own spotless soul. It's a good deal!

What St. Louis de Montfort and other saints, including the great "Marian pope" John Paul II, say is simply that the Total Consecration is the most perfect and efficacious way to "work out [our] own salvation in fear and trembling" (Phil 2:12). The scriptural basis for this, according to de Montfort is rather simple. How did Jesus Christ come to us? He came to us through Mary. If she is the perfect vessel to bring him to us, how then should we go to him? By that same perfect vessel, of course. De Montfort further explains, "As all perfection consists in our being conformed, united and consecrated to Jesus it naturally follows that the most perfect of all devotions is that which conforms, unites, and consecrates us most completely to Jesus. Now of all God's creatures Mary is the most conformed to Jesus. It therefore follows that, of all devotions, devotion to her makes for the most effective consecration and conformity to him. The more one is consecrated to Mary, the more one is consecrated to Jesus"[23]

De Montfort also notes many specific blessings which come to us if we come to Christ this way, which are too numerous to list here.[24]

Although I am still very much a work in progress, I can honestly say that I have experienced the great fruits of this consecration, particularly in the area of scrupulosity and servile fear. Growing up, what motivated my spirituality was the fear of hell more than the love of God. Over the years, as my relationship with the Lord Jesus Christ grew deeper, I began to see more and more his great love for me. The scrupulosity faded and was gradually replaced by a sense of true freedom and true confidence in his love for me.

Shortly before I submitted this book to the publisher for editing, I again renewed my consecration to Our Lady, but this time, I also specifically consecrated this book and any future mission which would emanate from it. More importantly, I asked my wife and children to also consecrate themselves with me. The experience has been nothing short of amazing as I watched Our Lady transform them, heal them, and help them grow in virtue almost overnight!

Of course, our experience is hardly unique. Many people who are a *lot* holier than us also consecrated themselves in this way. In fact, many of our great modern saints did it. Among the most notable, of course, is St. John Paul II. Another great saint was St. Maximillian Kolbe, who was

---

[23]   Ibid., nos. 120, 157.
[24]   Ibid., nos. 213–22.

martyred in the Nazi concentration camps, and of course, who could forget the St. Teresa of Calcutta? The fruits are simply undeniable.

Blessed indeed is the fruit of her womb and not only Jesus Christ but all those who would be sanctified by him and thus become her spiritual children, to whom he says, "Behold, your mother!" (Jn 19:27).

Naked Without Shame

Nakedness.

In today's sex-obsessed society, it is a word that usually has erotic connotations. In the beginning, however, the Holy Scriptures tell us that this was not always the case. In Genesis 2:25 we read, "And the man and his wife were both naked, and were not ashamed."

Doesn't that sound incredible? That was really the way it was supposed to be. Nakedness is really the expression of one's maleness or femaleness; nakedness without shame is the person's acceptance of his or her own sexuality as God created and intended. Due to the fall of man and our inherited concupiscence, or tendency to sin, this primordial meaning has become horribly twisted and therefore clothing becomes necessary in order to uphold our human dignity.

One of the famous sayings of John Paul II, which he repeated throughout his pontificate, was, "Be Not Afraid!" as noted at the beginning of this book.

That was a constant theme in my journey toward wholeness; I had to conquer my fears of being "unlovable" by men. In a certain sense, when we are able to truly open ourselves up to another and have that kind of intimacy together, we become "spiritually" naked and vulnerable with each other. It is a true friendship when you can look at each other with all the flaws and imperfections exposed and still love each other without feeling a sense of shame.

For me, that also meant overcoming my fear of being physically naked in front of another man. I had always been so insecure with my own nakedness. Since I had resolved so many years ago to keep my "deep, dark secret" to myself, I didn't partake of anything where I would have been physically, emotionally, or spiritually vulnerable with another man, including my own father.

I never had the proverbial "locker room" experience. I would never have allowed myself to be seen by another man in a state of undress, nor would I have looked at another man's nakedness. What if I had an erection? What if I looked too long? The other problem is at that point I still had true erotic attraction to the bodies of men. I say the bodies of men because I never got close enough to know them as people. I viewed men from a distance, as objects to be desired—idols, if you will.

When I was first checking out Franciscan University, there was a time which forced me to overcome my fears and do just that. The university had a program called "Come and See," where the prospective student was invited to spend a weekend on the campus living in the dorms, courtesy of the university. One weekend, I decided to drive the six-plus hours out to the university to see if that was where I really wanted to be. When I arrived, I had been assigned to the dorm known as Saint Francis Hall.

I roomed with two awesome guys who just by being themselves were the best ambassadors the school could have found. I was having a great time until I went to the bathroom. I was horrified to find that there were only common showers, no individual booths.

"Holy cow!" I thought in a panic. *"My secret is bound to get out and it will be all over for me here before it even starts!"*

So, the first night, I planned my shower at a time when I knew the bathroom would be empty. I wasn't so lucky on Sunday. I had to shower before Mass and the bathroom was full of naked men showering together, laughing and talking and having a great time. *I had no choice!*

In I went. I was actually so scared and stressed out that there was no possible way I would ever have an erection. God had saved me . . . that time.

When I came out of the shower, I confessed to the guys I was staying with that I was a little uncomfortable with the shower situation and asked how they felt about it. They first told me that none of the other dorms on campus had this style of shower. They also admitted that they had also been uncomfortable at first but then told me that after a while, they realized it really built a sense of camaraderie and trust among the men.

One of them said very straightforwardly, "That's why Saint Francis Hall never loses an intramural football game."

To my knowledge, his statement was true.

During the years I later attended the university, they actually renovated Saint Francis Hall. When the residents found out that the new plans removed the community showers in favor of individual stalls, there was no small protest.

Whether that story is true or not, Saint Francis Hall no longer has that shower arrangement. In a sense, it is sad. I have often wondered if I could have received a deeper, faster healing if I had been able to confront my fears and experi-ence true masculinity like that during my formative years.

Once I finally arrived at the university, I had another experience which continued my healing. During spring break, the university offered a program called SonLife in which students could travel to Florida together. While most spring break trips focus on partying, it had a different focus for Steubenville students. We did go to the beach in Florida, but to evangelize rather than to party.

We stayed in a retreat house run by a group of nuns. The basic program was that we would get up in the morning and have breakfast and Mass together. Next, we all boarded a bus and headed down to the beach for the day where we would perform skits, lead public games, and do one-on-one beach evangelization. This was my first time being on a beach with a bunch of Catholics my own age.

At the end of one of the days, a bunch of the guys had an impromptu wrestling match on the beach, so I joined in. Neither I nor the other guy was wearing anything except a bathing suit. I had a lot of anxiety just thinking about it, but I figured, what the heck.

I found out two things.

First, I was not very skilled and got quickly pinned. Next, I found that I really liked it, not in an erotic way, but more the physicality of it. I enjoyed the competition and phys-ical connection provided by the sport. This gave me some insight into understanding the psychology of sports, which had always been very foreign to me.

After we returned to the retreat center, since our cabins were single-sex and there were lines for the shower, most of the guys disrobed completely and stood in the line laughing and talking about the day. I figured it was now or never. Off went my clothes as I joined the line. There was something very freeing about it. The guys weren't even focused on nakedness but rather on each other and on the day. It was another "locker room" experience, and it gave me a sense of oneness with the men I was with. I began to see them not as mysterious and distant but more like me than I had ever realized before.

Again, my fears about my own nakedness were unfounded. I had taken the next step toward wholeness. The grace of the Lord, as always, was sufficient.

And there was more to come.

Naked and Unafraid

B esides shame, there was still another consequence of the Original Sin. Recall that Adam and Eve were both naked and felt no shame either in being naked before God or before each other. That all changed after the Fall. Adam used to walk through the Garden of Eden with God and never even gave his nakedness a second thought. Now, after the Fall, look at how the relationships change in Genesis 3:8–10: "And they heard the sound of the LORD God walking in the garden in the cool of the day, and the man and his wife hid themselves from the presence of the LORD God among the trees of the garden. But the LORD God called to the man, and said to him, 'Where are you?' And he said, 'I heard the sound of thee in the garden, and I was afraid, because I was naked; and I hid myself.'"

Now, after their sin, the primordial couple is not only ashamed of their nakedness with each other but also with their Creator. When God asks Adam where he is, he is not trying to figure out their physical location. He obviously knows that.

Adam has left him and he almost mournfully asks where his beloved creature has gone, not physically but spiritually. Besides shame, another element has also crept into the picture: fear.

They are not only ashamed but also afraid, which causes them to run and hide their nudity. This ancient flight away from the Creator and one another, motivated by fear and shame, has reverberated tragically throughout the ages of fallen humanity.

I had taken my first steps toward healing my shame, and next, I would take steps toward healing my fear of my own nakedness before other men. One of my household brothers helped me to see this more clearly.

The first time I ever saw Al was at that first Household Life Mass. He was one of the men I noticed there but I really didn't get to know well until my second year of household. It was during that year that a bunch of other brothers and I rented a dilapidated old mansion in downtown Steubenville.

Consistent with being Knights, we affectionately (and we thought, rather cleverly) dubbed the old stone house "The Castle." In reality, it was really a pitiful, decrepit building with "character," but no one in his right mind would have lived there voluntarily except for a bunch of college guys. So there were between eight and ten of us living there at any given time, and it became the household headquarters off campus. Al was one of the Knights who eventually moved in.

Al is one of those men who is blessed with a truly masculine spirit. He exudes manhood—not "machismo" but true manhood. In college, he was strong, athletic, intelligent, confident, and gentle—a true "Renaissance man" with a deep love for God and God's will in his heart. His spirit is very large and he naturally draws other men to himself. It was through my interactions with Al that very tangible signs of my sexual healing came.

One day, Al asked me if he could talk to me about something that was weighing very heavily on his heart.

He seemed very distressed. He closed the door behind him and proceeded to tell me of a relative who was currently involved in a homosexual relationship. He was having some difficulty in coming to terms with it and wanted someone to talk to who might be able to offer insight. I assumed he wanted to talk to me because he knew I was most of the way through my master's in counseling because I had never told him about my struggle nor, by his own later admission, did he have any reason to believe that I had struggled with this issue.

After several hours of listening to him share the pain in his heart, I finally let him in on my secret and offered him any insights I could on how best to approach the situation. While it felt good to again share, when I woke in the morning, I felt uncomfortable and nervous.

It suddenly dawned on me that since we lived in the same house, we naturally see each other in various states of undress. We had a very large bathroom almost like a small locker room, which made it possible for several of us to get ready at the same time. He is a few years younger, so I worried about how he (or even I) would feel when I saw him without clothes or semi-clothed again.

It happened that the next day we ended up in the bathroom at the same time. I had just gotten out of the shower and was about to dress when he came in. We exchanged morning greetings and he proceeded to undress as we chatted. Although the moment was only seconds, a healing occurred then. This man, this brother of mine, trusted me enough to be in the same room, in close corners with neither of us wearing a stitch, with him being fully aware of my struggles.

This was one of the few times during the healing process that I actually felt something give inside me, almost like a snap. The joy that bubbled up almost made me laugh. He didn't seem aware of how deep this was for me at the time, but his gift to me is one that I have never forgotten. Just having him accept me in both my literal and spiritual nakedness was incredible beyond words. Allowing me to do the same for him was another brick in the divinely reconstructed edifice of my masculinity. It was the most profound of all "locker room" experiences.

I still keep in touch with Al. One day, many years after this experience, he called me. It had been several months since we had last talked. We live on opposite sides of the country and, with the demands of family life, sometimes we end up playing phone tag for months.

We finally connected, and after catching up on old times and getting the updates, I decided to ask Al if he remembered that day in the bathroom. At first, his recollection was vague, but then when I described the whole scene for him, he remembered.

"I don't even know if you were aware of how much that meant to me," I told him. "I just need to thank you for doing that for me. You helped make me the man I have become. I appreciate the trust you placed in me."

He answered, "At the time, for a brief second, when I saw you in the bathroom, I did have some hesitation, but something inside told me that God was working in you. I trusted you with my body and knew that you would not do anything to compromise my dignity as a man and as your brother. I just knew that the Holy Spirit was on you and there was nothing to worry about."

I responded, "I feel the same way about you. I knew I was taking a risk when I talked to you that night, and at that time, you were the only household brother I had told; I had no idea how you'd react, but I also felt that abiding presence of the Holy Spirit on you. I knew I could trust you too."

I then went on to tell Al all my observations about him. I told him that he was one of the first Knights I had seen when I arrived onto the campus at that Household Life Mass.

"From the first time I saw you, somewhere deep inside, I knew you were my brother," I told him.

After I had said all this, there was silence on the other end.

I asked him if he was okay, and he said he was but that he was a bit humbled by all the things I told him.

"You know," he said, "all the things that you said to me about my helping you to grow as a man, you have also done for me."

This was actually somewhat of a surprise to me because I didn't often see myself as being able to minister to "masculine" men with my own past struggles. There is a tendency that I have to fight in myself that I see myself as "not man enough" or maybe too intense for most men.

But Al continued on, "I have a lot of friends, but there are really very few that I have the depth that I have with you. I need you to know that I have messed up a lot on my own sexual life and I've done some things that are wrong and I'm not too proud of that."

He then went on to explain a lot of his own struggles with his sexuality and with addiction. Now it was my turn to be humbled. What Al told me was nothing surprising. I already knew he wasn't perfect and probably fell into the sins that most men fall into. But what was so awesome was that he trusted me enough again to tell me his weaknesses and know that I would not use those against him but rather to build him up and help him walk the walk as a brother as he had done for me.

This is what true love between men is. It's not something erotic or self-serving but, rather, something strong, pure, holy, deep, unpretentious, honest, and intimate.

When he was finished, I thanked him again for trusting me and said, "I need you to know two things. First, none of this is surprising or shocking to me. Second, it doesn't change my opinion of you. It only makes you more real, more human. Your manhood is not in where you fall but where you rise again and continue walking with the Lord. That's what I love about you, Al. You know beyond a shadow of a doubt that God loves you no matter how you fall and you let that love shine through you."

After a few seconds of silence, Al asked, "You know what?"

"What?" I replied.

"I love you, brother," he said.

Without hesitation I answered, "I love you too."

Al went on to confirm a pattern in my life when I tell my story to whomever the Holy Spirit inspires me.

He said, "Your story and your struggle help me to hang on when my own cross seems so heavy to bear."

This is what so amazes me about Our Lord. When most men hear my story, they often see a validation of their own struggle and an idea of just how great the healing power of Jesus Christ is. I thought that when I told my story that many men would be insecure knowing what I have been through and where my weaknesses are. Just the opposite is true, in most cases.

Again, the Lord was repeating the same theme in my life that the path of my own personal holiness was not in spite of my SSA but *in and through it* and that he would continue to lead me and others to holiness through that cross.

Although Al, like most men, never suffered with same-sex attractions, he still found in my story strength for his own sexual struggles. He told me that if God could heal me so profoundly, then Christ's grace really is sufficient, as St. Paul says, and that chastity and purity are *real* possibilities for all men. The grace of Jesus Christ really *is* that powerful, and that holy cross really *is* the instrument of salvation.

My experience with Al obviously had a profound effect on me because it was precisely through trusting another man with my "nakedness," both physical and spiritual, that I grew so much in faith.

Living with my brothers had closed that distance for me and united the body with the spirit in my own mind. As St. John Paul II taught in his *Theology of the Body*, "The body, in fact, and only the body, is capable of making visible what is invisible: the spiritual and the divine. "[25]

Not only was I naked and unashamed, but naked and *unafraid*.

---

[25]   John Paul II, *Man and Woman He Created Them: A Theology of the Body* (Boston, MA: Pauline Books and Media, 2006), no. 19.4.

"He Loved Him as His Own Soul"

Once I began my healing process and continued to grow in chaste but intimate friendships with men and got out of sinful thoughts, patterns, and actions, the desire for sexual acts with men gradually diminished. Most times, the only thing left was a still strong desire for affection, tenderness, and intimacy.

At first, I thought that these desires were part of the "gay" package and something to overcome. However, once I understood my needs and desires for what they actually were, I grew to see that they were actually a part of who I am.

Something must be made very clear at this point. Both the *Holy Bible* and the Catholic Church condemn only same-sex genital acts and lustful, sinful behaviors that may lead up to it as mortally sinful. Neither has ever condemned emotional intimacy, tenderness, chaste "brotherly" physical affection between two men so long as these expressions do not lead to sinful thoughts or behaviors. Thus, there is no condemnation of friendship, even strong, loving friendships between two men.

Adding to the confusion, however, in the United States and some other countries, our culture does not permit strong, affectionate male friendships as socially acceptable. They are viewed through the societal lens as "gay" by most.

This is not the case in some other cultures throughout the world.

Even the *Holy Bible* records the friendships between some men as being very intense and close. A passage in the book of Samuel puts forth David and Jonathan as an example of a strong friendship between two men. "When he had finished speaking to Saul, the soul of Jonathan was knit to the soul of David, and Jonathan loved him as his own soul. And Saul took him that day, and would not let him return to his father's house. Then Jonathan made a covenant with David, because he loved him as his own soul" (1 Sm 18:1–3).

The entire account of their friendship can be found in chapters 18–20 of the first book of Samuel, with the death of Jonathan and David's reaction recorded in the first chapter of the second book of Samuel.

Now, Jonathan was the crown prince and son of King Saul, the first king of the united twelve tribes of Israel. Anointed by the great prophet Samuel and selected for the position by the Almighty himself, Saul, nonetheless, grew drunk on his own power and fell into sin on numerous occasions until, finally, God had had enough and told Samuel to appoint a new king in Saul's stead. The Lord chose a young, rugged, handsome, and bold shepherd named David, of the house of Jesse of Bethlehem, whom the Lord calls "a man after his own heart" (1 Sm 13:14).

David also eventually falls into sin too, but unlike Saul, he always repents and humbles himself before God. Knowing David's ultimate love for him, God cuts off the lineage of the House of Saul and bestows it on that of David. Saul is told that his descendants will never follow him in ascending

Israel's throne, and this makes him bitter towards God's newly anointed.

When David also proves himself to be a cunning and brave warrior, even exceeding Saul's military prowess, Saul becomes enraged and begins to hunt David down in order to kill him.

There is one problem, though. Jonathan, Saul's son, strikes up an intense and loyal friendship with David as is here related in 1 Samuel:

> And Jonathan stripped himself of the robe that was upon him, and gave it to David, and his armor, and even his sword and his bow and his girdle. . . .
>
> And as soon as the lad had gone, David rose from beside the stone heap and fell on his face to the ground, and bowed three times; and they kissed one another, and wept with one another, until David recovered himself. Then Jonathan said to David, "Go in peace, forasmuch as we have sworn both of us in the name of the Lord, saying, 'The Lord shall be between me and you, and between my descendants and your descendants, forever.'" (18:4; 20:41–42)

Here's the clincher. This is what David says after Jonathan is tragically killed. "I am distressed for you, my brother Jonathan; very pleasant have you been to me; your love to me was wonderful, *passing the love of women*" (2 Sm 1:26 emphasis mine). Surpassing the love of a woman? Seriously? Are we sure they weren't secret lovers?

It is easy to see how many in the gay rights movement try to use passages like these to support their argument that the Bible blesses and encourages homosexuality. Really though, this is far from the case, but in our oversexualized society, it's an easy mistake to make. Read the passages more closely. In these passages lies the true model of masculine friendship.

First, we really need to establish what a truly "manly" friendship is *and what it is not*. The first thing we see is that Jonathan loves David "as he loved his own soul." He literally stakes his life on his love for David. He knows that his own father is out to kill David.

He also knows that David is God's newly-anointed and will eventually replace Saul as king. Jonathan knows that because of this *he* will never be king and *neither will his children*! Yet he still professes his love for David and aids him in escaping that wrath of King Saul. It is quite possible that Jonathan even put himself into danger by coming this close to David, considering the depth of Saul's irrational and blinding anger.

David, for his part, reciprocates this love by bowing down before him three times. So here's the future king bowing down to the crown prince of the current rival king. David also takes a risk in entrusting himself to the son of his enemy. What if Jonathan were to deliver him into Saul's hands? Could he really be trusted? Nonetheless, trust him David does, and at least partially through Jonathan's patronage and with his help, he eventually escapes Saul's wrath.

So both David and Jonathan place the needs of the other above his own. This is true love. This is the love that two brothers who battle together share, and this is the love by which, as the Scripture notes, "iron sharpens iron" (Prv 27:17). This is also the key to understanding David's agony over the death of Jonathan and when he says that Jonathan's love was somehow above the love of women.

Rightfully, most modern readers are uncomfortable with that statement, and if taken in isolation, it could, to the modern mind, tend to support the idea that David and Jonathan were gay lovers.

Nothing could be further from the truth.

All the ancient writers were well aware of biblical proscriptions against sex between men. They certainly never would have written down such an embarrassing detail about their beloved king (even if were true!) which could be so widely interpreted (and misinterpreted) unless they had a different understanding of what was meant by the episode.

So what is the correct understanding of this passage, and if these two were not gay lovers, what could David's disturbing declaration mean? The answer is actually very simple. Recall that a man's true mission is to serve. To serve means to give of one's self, even to the point of giving one's own life, as Christ did. The problem is that men cannot give what they do not have.

Wives, children, families, and careers take from men. It's not wrong; it's just what happens. It is the way of a man's salvation. The woman's role is to receive the man, both physically and emotionally. He must give himself in order for her to receive. But how can he give from his own cup if his own cup is empty? This is where godly male friendships come into play.

Only a man can give another man what he needs to serve.

Only a man knows what another man truly needs simply because he is a man.

A woman, no matter how sympathetic, grace-filled, or holy, cannot know what it is like to be a man. Despite the fact that women give themselves in so many other unselfish ways (most times, way better than men!), they cannot give themselves to a man the way a man can.

True friendship and Christian brotherhood between men is *exactly* what Jonathan and David had. They demonstrated true vulnerability towards each other and shared their hopes, dreams, and fears. When they had emptied themselves out, they stood before each other spiritually naked and *weak*. It is in what happens next that the essence of masculine love is shown. They don't use this mutual vulnerability to manipulate or control the other. Instead, they defend and build each other up afterwards.

They *love* each other the way only men, as true brothers, can.

They make a masculine gift of self to the other through the heart and will, but *not with their bodies*.

I admit that when I read this account, it does bear a lot of similarities to a committed same-sex relationship. It *should*.

Again, neither Jesus Christ, the Bible, nor the Church ever condemned two men truly loving each other. The Gospels tell us that Jesus Christ himself loved his apostles. John rested his head on the chest of Jesus at the Last Supper.

There is nothing wrong with men expressing themselves with one another physically, but they are supposed to do it in the way that God intended. Sexual acts are just not a part of that and never will be.

The real key to understanding this passage appears as the title of this chapter: *he loved him as he loved his own soul.* Does that sound familiar to you? If you are a Catholic or other Christian, it should. These are the words of Jesus Christ himself!

Did he not explicitly *command* that we love one another as we love our selves? Did he not say that upon this and its corollary command to love God above all else rests the entire Law and the Prophets?

Here it is! The true Gospel proclaimed by the Almighty Son of David, practiced a millennium before him by David himself. This is the very love that Jesus wants all of us to have for each other! This *is* the Gospel!

True male friendship is not just in accordance with the proclamation of the Gospel, it *is* the Gospel, in the sense that the Gospel is about love of neighbor. We are called to love each other wholly. How do we do that? Look at David and Jonathan. They found that other trusted man before whom they could bear all and each knew that the other would protect and defend him.

How does this play out in modern life?

I would imagine that many men have not found this kind of friendship mainly because they are afraid to go there and also because, honestly, as the saying goes, a good man is hard to find. We can't just go around revealing ourselves to just anyone. Not everyone is worthy of our trust. One of the benefits of my struggle is that I have found not just one but several Jonathans.

I met my friend Owen in 1997 at the same prayer group where I met Josh. Owen is one of my closest friends. We have known each other for many years, through our ups and downs and everything in between. We have many similarities in our lives and how we see the world. Over the years, our friendship developed based on our common love for Jesus Christ and his Church.

I have been vulnerable with Owen like I have not been with any other man. Over time as our brotherhood grew stronger, we gradually shared all the depths of our hearts, even the dark parts. I think we know and love each other to the greatest amount that any two men could, like Jonathan and David.

We have shared things with each other that only our wives know.

We have shared our sufferings, trials, joys, and dreams.

We have held each other and wept in each other's arms when the pain of our own lives seemed insurmountable and our crosses too great to bear alone.

We have shared our relationship with God and prayed each other through the discernment of marriage, jobs, and vocations. In short, we've seen it all in each other and have still been there to defend and build each other up.

We love each other as the God-given brothers we never had.

Unlike me, Owen does not struggle with same-sex attraction, which was great for me. Nearly all of the men in my life with whom I have a deep intimacy do not share my same struggle. This is good on a variety of levels, the most important of which is that I don't have to worry about falling into temptation.

Additionally, finding men who are different from me yet can love me still helps me to know that despite my rather circuitous sexual journey, I really am OK.

I really *am* a man made after God's own image.

I am *man enough*.

It is in precisely these relationships with men like Owen, Josh, Al, Isaac, and all the brothers in my life that I have learned my own true masculine strength.

One of these strengths is my capacity to even sustain these kinds of relationships at all.

Quite frankly, most guys I see do not even pursue this type of deep friendship with other men. Some may not know they need it, and still others probably don't need it quite as much. However, the one thing that all of my closest friends tell me in one form or another is that they have no other friends like me. They tell me how much they enjoy the intimacy of our relationship and how they just cannot talk to other men with the depth that they talk to me.

This was encapsulated in an email I received one day from a remarkable and faith-filled friend of mine. At the time, she was serving as missionary in Middle-Eastern countries. Indeed, the Lord has worked powerfully through her.

One day, she emailed that she was starting a group to minister to Muslim men with same-sex attractions in the country where she was residing. She noted that these men have very few resources because this sort of thing is just not talked about in Islamic culture. I felt called to share my struggles with her via email and to let her know that I'd be willing to serve as a resource for her if she should ever need me. Here is what she wrote back to me: "One thing I have learned about the men I know that have struggled through SSA . . . they are incredible! The love they have for their wives, the encouragement they give them, and the gift of friendship they give to others is fantastic! I think [men with SSA] become more sensitive to people's needs as a whole and are incredibly special."

This email really ministered to my heart because it summarized the discoveries I have made about myself over the years. My struggle really is the path of my holiness, not only mine, but those around me.

I used to run from my cross and hide from the shame of it.

It was something I wished would just go away. I mean, I just wanted to be *normal* like other guys.

But the truth is that the servant is truly no greater than the Master.

He joyfully accepted his cross. There was a time when I thought I could never accept it.

Yet now with this incredible band of brothers around me, I can truly say and mean, "Thank you, Lord, for this great gift—the gift of my cross."

I will often say to the men I love, "You made me the man I am."

And it is true, but I also know that the reverse is also true. By the sheer grace of God, the power of Jesus Christ, and the gifts he has given me to share, somehow I make them the men they are too.

As Catholics pray at the beginning of each station of the cross, "Adoramus te, Christe, et benedicimus tibi, quia per sanctam crucem tuam redemisti mundum."

"We adore you, O Christ and we bless you, *because by your holy cross*, you have redeemed the world."

Putting an End to Childish Things

So, over a number of years, I had gradually learned about and gained entry into the world of men and how to give and receive male love properly. Once I had solidified my own masculine identity through my relationships with men, the next logical step, with Our Lady's help, was to restore a proper relationship with women.

A journal entry from that time shows my struggle to allow myself to be "remade":

> While I am sure that I am being changed, I am gripped with so much confusion, isolation and anxiety. I know that I will never embrace a homosexual lifestyle. I can't; it's just not acceptable to me. I am starting to see the beauty of the feminine and homosexuality plays a much less significant role in my life. I want to marry so badly and it hurts so much.

So, despite all the great things the Lord was doing in my life, the experiences I was having and all the people I was meeting, even in the midst of all this, I experienced a profound loneliness during this time. In many ways, most young adults who have not yet settled on a vocation in life experience this, not just those who struggle with SSA. They grapple with questions like: "Will I ever meet someone I can marry?" "What is the purpose of my life?" "What is God's will for me?"

For a man with SSA, I think this pain and loneliness is even more intensified. Since I had grown up identifying with women instead of men, the roles were, in a sense, reversed. I used to feel like "one of the girls," rather than "one of the guys," so the world of women seemed familiar to me while the world of men seemed so mysterious and alluring and, at the same time, frightening. What I thought was a great familiarity with women on which I had prided myself had actually prevented me from experiencing the true "feminine mystique."

Yet, despite my backwards perception and socialization, something within me now found women attractive, although not the sensual, erotic, and *consuming* way that I found a man attractive.

I dated periodically throughout the years, thinking that if I dated, I would somehow get over this "gay" phase. Actually, nothing could be further from the truth, at least not with men for whom the SSA is deeply ingrained, as it was for me.

It is true that the love of a woman probably can help heal homosexuality eventually, except for the fact that the problem is often started with incorrect relationships with women to begin with, so if a man with strong, unresolved SSA marries a woman, he really should be aware of these issues going into the marriage, if marriage is advisable at all.

If these issues *with men* are not at least *basically* resolved before marriage, he runs the risk of perpetuating his twisted view of sexuality and may actually exacerbate the SSA, often at the expense of the marital relationship. An SSA man's relationships with *men* need to be addressed before he can hope to give himself as a man to a woman. He cannot give what he does not have.

Now, I'm not saying that every last vestige of attraction to the same sex has to be completely gone. The degree of healing varies from man to man. Some men may never heal enough to have a healthy, heterosexual relationship. Others, like me, will heal to the point of being able to see same-sex attractions as the result of insecurity and hurt and still have a happy, fulfilling, heterosexual marriage. Still other men may be so completely healed that they "forget" their SSA and move on.

I didn't know that until much later on, so I ended up having some dating experiences that were less than what they should have been. A lot of times, the dates were just innocent fun where a girl and I would go out as "just friends." I actually enjoyed these platonic relationships because there was no pressure to act "like a man."

Although I was primarily attracted to men, when I occasionally did find a woman attractive, I would avoid any kind of interaction with them because their femininity always highlighted my own perceived lack of masculinity. I just always felt like a little boy with them if I was trying to function in any sort of masculine way or had sexual feelings. So the thought that went through my head constantly, whether I was consciously aware or not, was, "I'm not man enough."

This seemed to be the predominant way I dealt with all of my relationships, whether with men or with women. My own spirit was so shrunken. Did I see this at the time? No, not clearly. But it seems perfectly obvious now. This was highlighted for me through some incidents that happened in college.

Back then, I was selected to be a part of program which was basically a hand-selected group of pretty dynamic students who were hired to "sell" the school by giving tours to prospective students and their parents as well as run freshmen orientation once they did enroll. It was a mixed group of men and women.

I just did not have the capacity to relate to the men. Some of them actually did reach out to me, but I was so self-enclosed that I did not respond in a way that was appropriate. I was either too distant or too close, yet I secretly longed to be part of their world or even to *be them*.

With the women, it seemed like they pitied me because I was a pretty "off" kind of guy. I remember one incident, in particular, where we were preparing to put on a skit for incoming freshmen. In typical boy humor, which I totally didn't understand then, I remember some of the guys in the group trying to be funny and making lewd, sexual comments toward me. They weren't trying to hurt or make fun of me, just trying to "mix it up" in typical guy fashion, but what was more striking was the response from one of the women. She actually tried to protect and nurture me, as if my feelings would be hurt by what these guys were saying.

It would have been a touching scene were I not so pathetic that I didn't know to defend myself or, better yet, *actually engage with those guys*. I don't blame her at all; she was handling it in a very feminine way. The most emasculating thing was that this is the way a woman would relate to another woman, not a man! But that was just the reaction I elicited from people back then. My own weak masculine identity caused a vicious cycle in my interactions with others that more or less reinforced this weakness and my "gay" identity.

My lack of knowledge about the social interactions of men and women also extended to the dating and romantic planes. First of all, I wasn't even sure if I *should* date because of my attractions to men. This led to many internal conflicts on my part and also to many disappointments. I made a lot of mistakes.

I particularly remember one painful experience where I took a woman to a semi-formal dinner dance in college.

She was absolutely *gorgeous*!

It took all the confidence I could muster to ask her out, and once she accepted, I was elated and terrified at the same time. I didn't know what to do or how to act. I mean, I was always a nice guy and always treated people well, I just didn't treat men like men and women like women.

The night arrived and this woman looked radiant as always. I gave her a corsage and we boarded the bus for dinner. All went fairly well at dinner. I was still uncomfortable inside, but she seemed to be having a good time . . . until the bus ride home. We all boarded the bus, and since it was a college party with an open bar, many people were inebriated. It was stuffy on the bus, so we had let down all the windows to let in some cool spring air.

That wasn't the only thing that came in.

A few seats ahead of us, apparently somebody's date had consumed a little more liquor than he could handle. The next thing we knew, there was vomit spewing through all the windows. It flew through the air and landed on all of us, including my date, soiling her coat.

I apologized but did nothing else. I didn't offer to take the coat to be cleaned or even to pay for the dry cleaning. I didn't confront the guy (or at least his date, whom I would have known well) to ask him to apologize (and maybe pay for the coat to be cleaned).

In short, I did not behave *like a man*.

I was just too frightened and honestly didn't know what to do. I can't imagine what she must have thought of me, all of it well-deserved. Obviously, we never went out again.

Years later, after I had received much healing, I briefly dated another woman in my graduate program. Liz was a strikingly beautiful woman. We had an attraction almost instantly.

Although I still wasn't sure of how deep my healing went, I decided that since I found her so attractive, I'd give it a shot and ask her out. It was really unusual because I didn't feel like a little boy around her. So I got up the courage and she said yes!

We had a great time together and I learned a lot about how to treat women from her. I still didn't know that women need to be treated differently from men. This was probably a result of my 1970s upbringing and my lack of instruction and connection to the world of men.

Liz is a very talented artist, and as such, she instructed me on the art of dating very delicately and gently. I learned to open car doors and do the little things that make women feel special. I can't say I learned completely or quickly as I was definitely a work in progress, but Liz was patient with me and dedicated.

She was also my first kiss.

Yup, I was 22 and I had never kissed a woman . . . or a man for that matter. What can I say? There were a lot of reasons for this. Physically, I was a late-bloomer, and psychologically, I was too mired in my own issues to even approach that area. Another big part of the reason is that I didn't want to hurt any potential dating partner and drag her down into my own struggles. With Liz, I didn't seem to have those fears. I really grew a lot in our relationship and learned a lot about myself.

The one thing I always promised myself is that I would always tell any woman with whom the relationship had the potential to become serious about my struggles with my sexual identity. So after a few months, I told her about my past. She was very supportive and said that she had known a lot of men who struggled in this area. It was a definite healing and grace that she still accepted me and was willing to continue in our relationship.

The romance didn't last long, however, not because of my struggles but just because of the realization that we were two very different people with different goals. We just viewed the world too differently.

To begin with, Liz was over a decade older than me. Although I don't think this would have made a huge difference in the long run, she was definitely a lot more experienced in the ways of the world and I was still relatively young and naïve. Thus, we held differing expectations of what our relationship needed to be.

I think our biggest difference, though, was that despite our common faith in Christ, we had what the Church refers to as "disparity of cult." Liz was not Catholic, and despite her belief in Jesus Christ as her Savior and her active involvement on many levels of her church, she had no intention of becoming Catholic.

This was a problem for me since I knew that if I were to share the sacrament of marriage with a woman, I also needed to be able to share in the sacrament of the Lord's Body and Blood with her. There was no way in my mind that I could ever have the most intimate human relationship with a woman with whom I could not share the most intimate spiritual relationship. I needed something more in a life partner.

Thus, Liz and I mutually agreed that we would not date, but we still remained close friends during our time at the university. I personally grew a lot just from having such a positive experience with an older woman. I now knew that although insecure and far from perfect, with much to learn, I was "man enough."

I was reminded of what St. Paul says in 1 Corinthians 13:11, "When I was a child, I spoke like a child, I thought like a child, I reasoned like a child; when I became a man, I gave up childish ways."

I had finally begun to put away those childish things and to finally see (and like) myself as a man.

The Heart of a Woman

B esides Liz, I dated other women, but none of these relationships lasted. I always wanted things to work out, but then I would get caught up in overanalyzing myself and trying to decide if God were really calling me to marriage. I really wasn't sure if I was even capable of sustaining a heterosexual relationship yet. As of yet, I still did not feel like I truly understood the complementarity of the two sexes.

I was also trying to see if God might be calling me to the priesthood. I never felt any internal inclination in that direction, but being my scrupulous self, I needed to really be sure of that.

During my time at Franciscan University, I was suddenly surrounded with hundreds of Catholic men and women, most of whom actually were striving to be holy. It helped put things in perspective for me. For the first time in my life, I didn't have anyone asking me if I had considered the priesthood, and I was with a group of guys who were all seeking God and most *were not* called to the celibate life. I wasn't really that much of a standout. I could actually focus on myself and my calling without a lot of external influences. At the end of my time there, I felt fairly certain that I did not have a vocation to the priesthood.

Ironically and providentially, I graduated from Steubenville on May 13 of the Jubilee year 2000, which is the liturgical feast of Our Lady of Fatima. It was also the same day that St. John Paul the Great released at least the first part of the Third Secret of Fatima. These were yet more signs for me that the Virgin Mother of Fatima was still very much present with me in my walk.

Of course, now that graduation was imminent, I had to seriously consider what I was to do with the rest of my life. It so happened that during a retreat, I met a good, holy woman who I will call Sophie. She was a theology major who would finish her degree that December.

We used to have the greatest discussions, and it soon became obvious that we were mutually attracted. So we started off slow by enjoying the few weeks I had left before I would return home. We had some really great times together and God really seemed present in our relationship.

There were a lot of little "coincidences" that made it seem like God was bringing us together. Her hometown was about half an hour from mine and she was planning to move back there when she finished her degree. We both shared a great admiration and love for the writings of John Paul II, particularly the *Theology of the Body*.

It was actually she who introduced me to the works of Christopher West, whose mission it was to bring John Paul II's work to the general public. I really received a lot of sexual healing from his explanations of St. John Paul's work.

It seemed perfect. We were both two marriage-minded adults who were on fire for Jesus Christ, we lived fairly close, and we really enjoyed each other's company.

I figured this was *it*.

This was the woman I was going to marry. What more could I want? She was Catholic, beautiful, holy, intelligent, educated, and loved Jesus Christ more than she loved me. Those were all the qualities I was looking for in a wife. Any normal person would have thought it was a no-brainer.

Yet something just wasn't right.

I wanted it to be right.

I tried to *force* it to be right.

But, somehow, deep down in my being, I just knew it wasn't.

I had no idea why it wasn't right; it *seemed* perfect.

Was I not healed enough? Was I not called to marriage? Was this God's way of telling me I should become a priest? These thoughts swirled in my mind over and over again as I re-examined and reinterpreted our relationship, my calling, and my intentions. I was in the Blessed Sacrament Chapel all the time, constantly bringing this inner turmoil to the Lord and seeking his direction.

Sophie could also sense that there was something missing. She also seemed to be searching for something more than what we had. After months of dating, our relationship still lacked a certain depth and intimacy. It was more like we were close spiritual friends rather than romantic partners. We were just not united the way I thought a couple discerning marriage should be united.

One of the things that cued me in that something was awry was the fact that she would often make spiritual retreats, to which I was never invited. It seemed to me that she preferred her time in prayer and meditation over the time she spent with me. Don't get me wrong; it is a good and holy thing to have that depth of relationship with God; it's just that a relationship of such depth is usually one where God asks for an undivided heart.

To me, it was not a relationship that she could share with both God and me. My idea of marriage had always been that there would be a three-way relationship between the spouses and God and that he would serve as a common foundation through which the two of us would share our love and grow together. I felt almost excluded from Sophie's relationship with God. She had her relationship with God, and I had mine, and the two never crossed.

The more I thought about it, the more it made sense, but I was living in denial. I still wanted this relationship to work out. It had seemed so perfect and this is where I made my mistake.

Rather than trusting in God, and going with the sense I had in prayer, I continued to try and "make it work." I put my all into our relationship, made plans, discussed the future, and continued in my denial. This all came to a head at a friend's wedding that we attended. As I watched the couple exchange their vows, the realization suddenly settled on me that I just couldn't do this anymore and that there was no way I could spend the rest of my life with this woman.

So I discussed my feelings with Sophie, and despite failings on both our parts, we agreed that it was best if we did not continue our relationship. I wish I could say that our relationship ended smoothly. It did not. Sophie was very hurt by what she perceived to be my lack of love and care for her, and our relationship was completely severed.

This was one of my great lessons about the depths of a woman's feelings and how we men need to be more aware of the things we say, even if they are not mean or abusive and even when we have the best of intentions. A woman's heart rests on our words in a way that most men (including myself) do not understand because we don't experience things quite the same way.

It was a hard lesson to learn—for me and for her.

"Let It be Done to Me According to Your Word"

Besides Sophie's pain, there was still the issue of my own discernment to deal with. I don't think I ever felt more confused after I broke up with her. I thought for sure that if I had messed up so badly with this great Catholic woman, there was surely no hope for me. Maybe all "daily Mass ladies" were right . . . I must be called to the priesthood.

This had actually been a question in my mind for years, and I had debated it back and forth. When I was struggling with homosexuality, the question of the priesthood (and even of marriage) necessarily took a back seat to seeking sexual healing. Here I was, seven years later, just out of a relationship that by human standards *should* have worked.

It was not that I wanted to be a priest; I really didn't. I mean, I admire priests; I love liturgy and the Holy Eucharist and am not ignorant of the great honor that a call to the priesthood entails and just how precious that call is in the sight of God, but I always felt that I wanted to be married and raise a family.

But with my scrupulous nature, I thought that it really couldn't be God's will if *I* wanted it. Therefore, God couldn't be calling me to marriage, yet I desired marriage with all my heart.

Nonetheless, when I would pray, go to Mass, or do anything spiritual, these thoughts about the priesthood would come into my mind. I would imagine myself in a Roman collar or in priestly vestments and it just didn't look right. Yet these thoughts just kept coming at me to the point where they were causing physical anxiety, not to mention sexual anxiety.

I had been heavily addicted to masturbation as a teenager and into my college and graduate school years, sometimes masturbating three to five times in a single day. By the time I began dating Sophie, I had rarely struggled with it; it simply ceased to be enjoyable for me. I think the idea of possibly getting married forced me to build up self-control within myself. I had actually gone without masturbating for a number of months.

This all came crashing down when we broke up. I was devastated. I had no idea what to do with my life or where to go next. I had a good job as a high school teacher and I knew that I could take care of myself, but I had no vocation goals; I could not see the big picture God had in store for my life. This frustration eventually manifested in extreme sexual tension and temptation until I finally succumbed.

It was on a Sunday morning, so despite feeling really ashamed of myself, I attended Mass. I obviously didn't receive communion, but after Mass, I asked my pastor, a wonderful and holy priest and a good family friend, if he could hear my confession. I think priests just know that when a young man seeks them out outside of regular confessional hours, it is usually because of some sexual sin. I have never encountered a priest who was unwilling to see me, even on such short notice and while other things were clearly going on.

Our pastor beckoned me over to some pews off to the side of the magnificent Baroque-Renaissance church, an artistic gem nestled in the heart of a declining city. As he sat down in his vestments, which he hadn't even had the time to remove after Mass was finished, I began to pour my heart out to him and told him all about the events of the past eighteen months and my frustration about what to do now, culminating in my sexual sin.

He listened carefully and after giving me some words of encouragement, he, in doing what he would do again later on, prophesied about my life.

He looked into my eyes and said, "You have followed the Lord Jesus all your life; he's not going to abandon you now. Have patience and trust in him, and he will show you the path."

There was that same word I heard many years before again in this same church from the lips of the saintly Maria Esperanza, "Paciencia!" *Patience!*

This time, the words were music to my ears. Although I still felt turmoil, I somehow knew it was going to be all right, and I had a feeling that something great and new was on the horizon for me. The problem was that I did not yet know what it was, so the anxiety more or less remained.

Finally, on Holy Thursday of 2002, this internal dialogue between me and God became too much for me and I blurted out loud to God, "No! I will *not* be a priest. Leave me alone."

At that moment, I burst into tears as I realized that I had uttered the satanic oath, the antithesis of Our Lady's cosmic consent.

Instead of her great YES in Luke 1:38, "Let it be [done] to me according to your word," I had said, "Let it NOT be [done] to me according to your word."

Once I realized what I had said, I just fell to my knees and started crying.

The Lord of the Cosmos, the Creator of all things visible and invisible, the Eternal Father had asked me to give him my whole life, and I had told him, "No."

It was Adam's sinful echo in my own soul, "I will not serve."

I pulled myself together and decided to go out for a run to clear my head. It was a warm balmy spring day, just perfect. So, in the bright sunlight, I professed my love again for this greatest and most humble of kings.

I repented of my arrogance and prayed to the Lord the following prayer, "You win, Father. All I have, you have given me. If you want me to be your priest, I accept your gracious gift. Just show me the way."

Once I had made this gift of total self-donation to Our Lord, immediately, a profound sense of peace and joy filled my being. That was it. Despite all my best efforts, the Uncreated Lord had won out.

I was going to be a priest.

I immediately began making mental inventories of my life and thought about my job and my family and how life would change for me. Would I enter the seminary right away? How long would it be before ordination? How would I pay my student loans? Although I didn't have answers to any of these questions, I nonetheless, for the first time, offered up my whole life to God, keeping nothing back for myself.

It was so significant that I had come to this decision on Holy Thursday, of all days. This is the day on which Catholics remember the night of the Last Supper, where Christ instituted the Holy Eucharist for the first time, the new Passover banquet of Christ's new covenant. This is the night in which Christ became the new Lamb of God, *par excellence*.

The Liturgy for the evening is appropriately called "The Mass of the Lord's Supper." It is also the day when Christ consecrated the Apostles as Christianity's first apostolic bishop-patriarchs, thereby establishing the sacred priesthood.

It is, in a sense, the "anniversary" of priestly ordination. So it was to this solemn liturgy that I went, fully expecting to embrace the priesthood. Indeed, I viewed Mass a totally different way than I ever had before; I didn't fight any of the images I had of myself in the collar or wearing vestments, or even celebrating the Holy Sacrifice of the Mass.

Yet, although I was filled with joy, there was still a part of me that wasn't quite convinced about this whole thing. By the time the Easter Vigil rolled around on Saturday, much of the initial eagerness and joy about the priesthood gave way to feelings of resignation. The thought of being a priest just didn't light my fire. I began to feel really confused all over again.

Why would God have given me such a feeling of joy when I just didn't feel like this is where I was supposed to be for the rest of my life? My prayer was still one of submission to his Holy Will, but I had lost that excitement.

My prayer was now, "Okay God, I'll become a priest . . . *if you really want me to.*"

It would turn out that this incident in my life was my Abraham moment, and the priesthood was my own personal Isaac. Like Abraham, it was what I needed to place on the Altar of Sacrifice, only to have the hand of God snatch the knife away before I went through with it.

Just a month later, God would tell me my true vocation and set me on the path to answer his call.

"I Am the Good Shepherd"

It was April 19 of 2002, in the middle of the Easter season. My parents were out of town for the weekend and my friend Judith was visiting. We had met in graduate school, were in the same program, and had both graduated back in 2000.

From the first moment I met Judith back in 1998, I was drawn to her. Here's what I wrote about her way back then:

> I am attracted to this girl in my class. I might even get up the courage to ask her out on a date. It feels so natural and I don't ever want this feeling to go away. I want to get to know her better. What is happening to me? Is this just wishful thinking? Yet, I have a profound sense of peace unlike any other. How can I feel this way so soon? I'm not completely over my homosexuality. Or am I? I don't know but whatever is happening here is good.

Indeed, I was not yet ready.

Neither was she.

It would be many years before the Lord got us to the point that we were both ready for each other. I had returned home to take a position teaching English (as per my undergraduate degree) at a public high school and Judith had opted to stay in Steubenville and eventually got a job there working as a

182

vocational counselor. It had now been two years since we'd left, and we had both led different lives and had different significant others, but we both stayed in touch periodically and continued the friendship we had started in our grad school years.

After I broke up with Sophie, I had called Judith, who had also broken up with her boyfriend at the time, to invite her to attend my cousin's wedding with me. I knew she would be great company, and it had been years since we had seen each other. She declined due to a previous commitment.

However, a few weeks later, she called me back to ask if I would accompany her to her aunt's wedding in New York. I told her I'd be delighted, and why didn't we just make a whole weekend out of it? She agreed and arrived on Friday night.

What happened next was solely the work of the Lord.

We traveled the two-plus hours from New Jersey to New York by car and the journey was just so comfortable and enjoyable. There was no pretense and no "trying." We just were—and we really enjoyed just being in each other's company. This was so different from all the relationships I had been in before. We rested on a solid friendship and the conversation just flowed so easily.

We finally arrived at the wedding and I met Judith's family and extended family. There was really nothing unusual about them except that I felt as if I belonged there! It wasn't as if I particularly even liked everyone there. In fact, there were some folks that I downright disliked, but all the same, there was still this abiding feeling that this was where I was supposed to be.

I knew it. I was sure. I *belonged* with her.

As if to confirm, one of Judith's relatives came up to me, stuck her index finger in my face, and with a thick Brooklyn accent said, "You! Marry her!" and pointed at Judith.

I couldn't help but laugh as I said, "OK!"

The thought of this filled me with joy and apprehension at the same time. It was similar to how I hear of people discerning what religious community is the right one for them. It just "feels like home."

It was a balmy but drizzly and misty day. Despite that, we opted to go outside for a walk. Up the river was a great view of the Manhattan skyline in the distance, minus the newly destroyed World Trade Center. I put my arms around her waist and we just stood there gazing off into the distance. There was such a feeling of peace and belonging. Our bodies just seemed to *fit* together. During the ride home, we really didn't talk as much as we had during the ride up, but that ease of comfort was still there.

The next morning was Sunday. Judith had to return to Ohio later that morning, so we decided to attend an early morning Mass. From the time I woke up, I felt nervous and jittery for no apparent reason. It wasn't a sense of foreboding but rather of anticipation, kind of like being a child on Christmas morning.

When we entered the church, I was overcome by a sense that I was going to marry Judith. It was that simple. I didn't hear a voice *per se*, but at the same time, I knew the Holy Spirit was whispering to my heart in the "still, small voice" that is God's. Despite my trepidation and anxiety,

I nonetheless managed to get down on my knees to pray before Mass started.

I prayed the following words, "Lord, I thank you for the vocation you have chosen for me."

That Sunday, unbeknownst to me, was the day set aside by the universal Church as "Vocations Awareness Sunday."

As if this weren't enough of a confirmation that this was the path God laid out before me, the Eternal Father made sure I knew that he was speaking to me directly. As Father (the same priest to whom I had confessed my trouble in discernment before) intoned the first prayers of the Mass and introduced "Vocation Sunday," much to my surprise, he then greeted the assembly with the *exact same words* I had just prayed saying, "Today is the day we *thank God for the vocation he has chosen for us*," he said.

I could have fallen over. *Word for word.*

Mass just got more and more intense for me. Besides the amazing confirmation of God's Word to me through the mouth of the pastor, there were more and more signs of God's outpouring of love and his almost palpable grace.

Weeks before, a friend of mine had been praying over me at our Men's Fellowship, specifically for direction in my vocation, and what he received in prayer was that I needed to be meditating and praying on Psalm 23. Guess what the psalm for that Sunday's Mass was? That particular Sunday was also *Good Shepherd Sunday*, which coincidentally (or Providentially) happened to coincide with Vocations Awareness Sunday that year.

The LORD is my shepherd, I shall not want. . . .

He leads me beside still waters;
he restores my soul." (Ps 23:1–2)

As the liturgy of the Church intends, the high point of my experience came with the Gospel when Jesus tells his followers about himself as the Good Shepherd, "I am the good shepherd; I know my own and my own know me. . . . My sheep hear my voice, and I know them, and they follow me" (Jn 10:14, 27).

I heard him!

I knew in the very depths of my being. It was not an audible voice, but I heard my Shepherd talking to me and telling me what he wanted me to do. His voice was so clear, so majestic, and so commanding, yet so quiet and unassuming. If I wasn't listening, I would surely have missed this holy whisper. But at that point, I was listening. *Thank God!*

Despite my initial fear and anxiety, I was now overcome by waves of joy and peace. It was so beautiful and so ecstatic that it brought tears to my eyes. I could scarcely contain myself. These feelings gave way to an excitement and exhilaration that nearly made me shake. It was so hard to remain attentive to the Mass.

I knew what I was supposed to do with my life!

The Lord had spoken and it would be so. This much I knew. The whithers and wherefores I knew not. I did not even know if Judith felt the same way about me, yet I had a great confidence that I had never known previously. This was it!

Little did I know that on the other side of the pew, Judith was having her own revelation. Unbeknownst to me, she was also getting a word from the Lord. The Lord was telling her that she would be married in this church. That's all he told her—she pieced the rest together herself.

Needless to say, the remainder of Mass and the breakfast that followed were filled with as yet unspoken thoughts and an intensity that almost made eating impossible.

Finally, the time came for Judith to return to Ohio. As we embraced by her car, I knew that we were destined to be married. As I held her there, I just didn't want to let her go, so I told her so.

She replied, "I don't want to go either."

I continued, "You know this means we have to get married."

"Yes," she said.

The Quest for the Hand
of My Bride

It really went like that.

In fact, I always joke around with people that I asked Judith to marry me three times. The time I just related was the first time, and after we realized what we were saying, we decided that we needed to take things more slowly and prayerfully.

Although it was several months before we became formally engaged, I just could not contain my joy. My heart was racing and my veins were pumping with adrenaline. I had to tell someone. I got on my cell phone and called Josh.

"Hello," he answered.

"Hey, man I got news for you. This is really sudden but I just want you to know that I'm getting married!" I told him.

He laughed out loud and said, "Are you serious?"

After affirming that I was, in fact, in my right mind, I answered in the affirmative.

"I didn't even know you were dating anybody!" he exclaimed.

"I really wasn't dating anyone. This is just what the Lord told me," I said.

I actually didn't even recall that dialogue until Josh brought it up as he was giving the toast at our wedding. Needless to say, it resulted in quite a round of laughter, but this memory really demonstrates two important things: the importance of discerning rather than "dating" as society commonly uses the word and the importance of having prayerful Christian friends who are used to listening to the promptings of the Holy Spirit and who have a solid prayer life.

The first point is exemplified by the fact that Judith and I only discerned for about two months before we decided to formalize our engagement. This is not a course of action I would recommend for most couples in today's society. In our case, we had known each other by hanging with the same mixed-group friends in graduate school. Without the pressure of "dating," we were able to be more relaxed and got to know each other for who we were, both good and bad, which formed the basis of a great friendship.

In the past, it was the role of families, who socialized with other families, often within the context of the church, to bring in "eligible" members of the opposite sex in larger social gatherings. Although the concept of the traditional family has been so eroded in our society, groups of friends can sometimes serve the same purpose.

Even before we had started dating, Judith and I had known each other for four years. We already knew the basics about each other and even some of each other's flaws as we got to know each other while we spent time with friends in our common circles. It sort of took the guess-work out of dating, so we were able to get down to discussing deeper issues faster.

There were a lot of those issues, particularly from our respective pasts, on both sides. Part of our growing process was sharing our painful wounds of the past with each other and discussing them together, out in the open. I told Judith about my past same-sex attractions very early on in our relationship.

On one end, in my heart of hearts, I knew Judith well enough and felt the Lord's call to marriage strongly enough to have confidence that she would not reject me. But on a purely human level, it was a very scary and uncomfortable conversation for me.

So I did it.

I told her all about my past and about my healing and where I was presently. I explained that I still sometimes felt insecure around and attracted to some men and was still working on forming my masculine identity, which although much stronger than before, still needed work and even more healing.

She could not have been more supportive. Her response was so incredibly affirming and truly reflected God's love for me. Judith is so rooted in her relationship to God that truly nothing shakes her if she believes that God is directing the situation. She asked a lot of questions and really tried to understand my struggles as best she could.

At the end of the conversation, she professed her love for me and her willingness to walk with me through any remaining difficulties I might have in this area. Given the emotional toll that sexual matters take on women, which men, as a rule, do not experience as profoundly, I knew that I was marrying an incredibly strong and holy woman.

It wasn't long after this conversation that our actual engagement process began to take shape. When we began dating and discerning that God was calling us to marriage, we had agreed that when Judith was ready, she would give me her mother's number so that I could drive up to her mother's house, which was in New York, about an hour north of Manhattan, roughly about two-and-a-half hours away.

I believe in the tradition of asking for the permission of the bride's parents, so I called Judith's mother and asked if I could drive up to visit and have lunch with her. Judith's father had died many years before, so only her mother could give the blessing. It was a fairly long day-trip in an area with which I was unfamiliar.

I'm not one of those people who enjoys driving to begin with, so the thought of driving in an unknown place by myself (through mountain roads, I may add) was not especially attractive to me. My sense of direction is not the greatest, and when I get lost, I really tend to stress out, and these were the days before GPS was so readily accessible.

Yes, I did get lost a couple of times and I did stress, and that coupled with the idea of asking someone's daughter's hand in marriage did not a relaxing ride make. Yet, it was another one of these journeys on which the Lord sent me where I had to travel again as a "foreigner" to an unknown land just like Abraham.

When I finally got there, I was pretty exhausted, excited, and nervous all at the same time. By this time, I had known my future wife's mother fairly well—this was one of the benefits of being in the same social circles. When our families came into town for a visit at the university, we also got to meet them, and get a broader picture of the person.

Although I knew Judith's mom, I was still a little scared. After all, we were getting engaged after barely three months of formal courtship. I don't know how I would feel if some guy wanted to marry *my* daughter that quickly. I did know, however, that Judith had been talking to her about our relationship, so this was not something that would blindside her. I thought she probably expected what was coming.

So I pulled into the driveway, walked up the steps, and took a deep breath. When she opened the door, we sat down and exchanged pleasantries for a while and I stated my purpose in coming.

She asked me a series of questions about how I planned to provide, and when she was satisfied, she then said, "Of course you have my blessing. Did you think I'd let you drive all this way if I didn't plan to give it to you?"

The rest of the time was fairly uneventful and we shared a pleasant afternoon lunch on the lake at the center of town. Driving home, I had the opportunity to reflect on the experience. In many societies, there are various "trials" that a man has to go through before he gets permission to marry a woman. It might be a certain amount of money he has to make or that he needs to have a house ready for her. For me, I had to place myself, if only temporarily, in a situation where I was not 100 percent comfortable. Afterwards, I felt really good about myself, like I had done the right and manly thing and made the quest for my bride.

A Special Gift From God

I wish I could say that the engagement was all smooth sailing, but it was not. My scrupulosity kicked in big-time. I guess it's something many men go through. The fear of commitment is just so great that there seems to be a time of just "freaking out." Even though I had clearly heard the Lord's voice on that Sunday morning, I still struggled with doubts as to whether I was doing the right thing. It wasn't that I had any doubts about Judith but rather doubts about myself.

Poor Judith. It must have been so hard for her to go through all that emotional turmoil from a woman's perspective, and it was getting to the point where I could no longer talk to her about it because I knew I was just hurting her.

So I focused all my energies on the discernment process. That is actually what engagement is for, traditionally. It is supposed to be a time of prayer and reflection as to whether God is, in fact, calling the couple together. And discern I did. I did a holy hour before the Blessed Sacrament each week and asked God to confirm my steps if I was walking in his way and to put up roadblocks if I was not. This is a really scary prayer because it meant abandoning my whole self to the Providence of God. I asked him to close the doors that were not in accord with his Will and open others.

In addition to my prayer, I also asked all the people who knew me best where they thought I was called. Gradually, my calling to marriage was more and more confirmed.

It was people saying things like, "I'm sure you'd make a fine priest, but that's not where I see you happiest."

Several of my friends in the Lord said to me that they did not think priesthood was my gift.

They all used that word, *gift*.

The hardest thing I had to do was ask my parents what they thought. I remember it clearly. I was in their kitchen agonizing over my discernment, so I finally asked my parents for their opinion. It was the same as all the rest.

With theirs, however, I experienced such a sense of relief that it brought tears to my eyes. I then did one of the most humbling things I have ever done. I asked for their blessing. I felt almost foolish doing it, but afterwards, I felt totally confirmed after they gave it. While my mother verbally gave it, my father (who had become more devout in later years) actually lifted his hand to make the sign of the cross over me. Even though we had such a rocky relationship, I still asked him and he willingly gave it. I still remember the impact of my dad's fatherly blessing on me even to this day.

Later, as I was in adoration, I received this Scripture from the Lord. I opened my Bible to 1 Corinthians 7:4–7, which reads:

> For the wife does not rule over her own body, but the husband does; likewise the husband does not rule over his own body, but the wife does. Do not refuse one another except perhaps by agreement for a season, that

you may devote yourselves to prayer; but then come together again, lest Satan tempt you through lack of self-control. I say this by way of concession, not of command. I wish that all were as I myself am. But each has his own special gift from God, one of one kind and one of another.

The gifts he writes about are the gift of marriage and the gift of celibacy. Paul is explaining why he remains celibate and why that is a good thing and also why it is also a good thing to be married. He echoes the Lord's words in Matthew 19:12 that anyone who can accept celibacy "for the kingdom" should but that very few people are actually called to this.

When I saw this text, it was as if these words jumped off the page and into my heart, rather like the old style movies where the director darkens the rest of the page so the viewer can see the text which he is trying to emphasize, "I wish that all were as I myself am. But each has his own special gift from God, *one of one kind and one of another.*"

At that moment, the Lord confirmed what everyone else had been telling me all along and these were the very words—celibacy is not my gift.

God didn't will me to be celibate.

Celibacy is not my gift.

Celibacy is not my gift!

WOO-HOO!

Saint John Paul II underscores this when he writes, "Thus, also those who choose marriage and live in it receive a 'gift' from God, 'their own gift,' that is, the grace proper to this choice, of this way of living, of this state. The gift received by persons who live in marriage is different from the one received by persons who live in virginity and choose continence for the kingdom of God; nevertheless it is a true 'gift from God,' a gift that is 'one's own,' destined for concrete persons, and 'specific,' that is, adapted to their vocation in life."[26]

Upon taking it even further into prayer, I also explored some of the reasons why I would have thought God was calling me to a life of celibacy even though he was clearly not. One was obviously the residual effects of my own homosexuality—my view of sex and what it meant was distorted and I had the mistaken notion that it was somehow wrong if I responded to sexual desire, even heterosexual desire.

Another reason for my angst was my own issues with scrupulosity—I always wanted to be sure that I *did* everything right to get to heaven. If I chose marriage, wasn't I, in a sense, rejecting God?

A final reason was a sense of pride on my part. I thought to myself that if there is such a priest shortage, I was obviously a young man of faith who could offer a lot to the Church. I didn't have any severe social issues, the sexual issues were resolving, I was orthodox and had a personal relationship with Jesus Christ. I was, overall, a pretty nice package. Why *wouldn't* God want me to be a priest? In my mind I was *a*, if not *the* perfect man for the job, right?

God didn't see it that way. He doesn't see as we see.

---

[26]   John Paul II, *Man and Woman He Created Them: A Theology of the Body* (Boston, MA: Pauline Books and Media, 2006), no. 67.8.

Marriage is truly my gift, and now all these years later, there has never been a single day when I ever regretted marrying Judith. Even during the hard times and the ups-and-downs inherent in every marriage, almost two decades, two houses, and three beautiful children later, I always had an abiding peace that I was truly where God called me to be and with my best friend in the world.

The wedding itself, despite its snafus, was like something out of a storybook.

It was a moment of pure grace and beauty.

The night before, Judith and I held a holy hour and confession at the rehearsal dinner where God gave us just so many graces. Among the greatest of these was that family members returned to confession who hadn't been for years just because we asked them to. Judith and I prayed together and specifically invited Jesus Christ to our marriage, not just on the wedding day itself, but on every day "till death do us part."

That day, as soon as I walked out into the sanctuary to receive my bride, it became apparent that the Lord had heard my prayers. The presence of the Holy Spirit in the church was palpable and intense. The graces were just pouring through every crack and crevice of the grand old edifice. It was like something out of *The Sound of Music* with the bishop waiting at the altar as our bridal party marched in to the instrumental version of the great Palm Sunday hymn "All Glory, Laud and Honor."

As I waited for Judith to come in, something happened in the vestibule which resulted in some confusion behind the closed doors. This led to a slight delay in Judith's entry, which caused dramatic suspense and anticipation in the congregation.

When the heavy wood doors finally swung open, the sunlight from outside suddenly flooded the back of the Church which gave the effect of her actually stepping out of the light and into the Church. It was so beautiful that some people gasped and wept with delight. I will never forget that first incredible moment when I saw my bride approach. It was indeed a great foreshadowing of the heavenly banquet of the Lamb described in the book of Revelation (19:9).

Our wedding guests who were believers already noticed and commented on how much they felt the presence of the Lord at our wedding. Even those of our wedding guests with little or no faith in Jesus Christ have told us that our wedding was so very different than other weddings they had attended. They described what they experienced as "joy," "peace," or "fullness." And indeed it was, and is.

Blessed be the Lamb.

"Therefore a Man Leaves His Father and His Mother and Cleaves to His Wife"

When Judith and I were first married, my SSA issues definitely rose to the forefront. Because of my own lack of formation in relationships, I caused my wife a great deal of suffering at the beginning of our marriage (and many times thereafter).

Although my family is Catholic, being products of the sixties and seventies, they were not the greatest examples of Christ-centered masculinity and femininity. Although good people whom I love, they didn't really strive to have Jesus Christ in the center of their lives and their relationships. So most of the modeling I saw was of people who didn't have a great grasp of things in this area themselves. It was very difficult to disengage from this and function as a Christian man in a Christian marriage.

So I made a lot of mistakes.

Perhaps one of the most hurtful of these happened on our wedding night. For reasons that I will more fully explain later, we could not consummate our vows on our wedding night, so we decided to go back to the room to undress and go to bed. Since I was still pretty wired from the events of the day and my wife was not, I innocently asked if we (or I) might go downstairs to the lobby to continue the party.

Bad thing to say.

I really wasn't trying to be hurtful but just didn't really get the depths of her heart.

I truly did not understand the depths of the emotions of women. Because of my lack of intimacy with men, I "hid" in the world of women, and although I thought I related to them more than men, I was ultimately seeing their world and relating to them through the eyes of a man.

So I really missed a lot!

I have written a lot about the issues I had with men in my family but have not yet really touched on issues with women. As is often the case with areas of sin in our lives, once we start working on one area, it is like peeling off layers and other areas come to the surface.

Besides a break with masculine society, the development of homosexuality often also rises due to relationships with women, especially the mother. It took me a lot longer to deal with my issues with women because the ones with men were so much more all-encompassing.

However, it may well be that issues with the mother and other women in the family go even deeper. It was years into our marriage (and because of it) that I really started to deal with issues with my mother.

These were issues that I didn't even know were there which were brought to light by my unconscious transfer of my feelings about the women in my family to my wife. It actually started on our honeymoon. As I mentioned before, we actually didn't consummate our marriage until a week or so after the wedding because we practice Natural Family Planning (NFP). This is a plan for regulating births which utilizes the woman's own cycles to try to delay (or as is often the case, to achieve) pregnancy.

Often confused with the "rhythm method," NFP aids the couple in finding the times during the month when the woman is most likely to be infertile if they wish to avoid pregnancy or those when she is most likely fertile should the couple wish to conceive. Without getting into all the scientific jargon, it is quite a beautiful way for the couple to communicate about their sexuality. Since we did not feel ready for a variety of reasons, we decided that we would postpone pregnancy. Unfortunately, Judith was fertile during the wedding, so we planned a Caribbean cruise for the following week.

One night, when the time was right, we were planning to do what honeymooners do. Since we were on a cruise, dinner was set at a specific time each night, and if you did not show up to the appointed time, you don't eat. So we got ready for dinner and had a couple of drinks to relax. My wife was ready for our first time.

Again, not wanting to miss the experience of the cruise, I suggested that we wait. An argument ensued which was fed mostly by the fact that I thought Judith was being manipulative and selfish to get what she wanted. I didn't realize then what I realize now, that when the woman says yes, at least in the area of sex, the man should just go with that.

Duh.

Rather than seeing this as the natural interplay between men and women, I saw it as a means of control. This was obviously quite hurtful to my wife, and even many years later, she recalled how painful it was.

Why did I think this way? With much prayer and reflection, I think that my upbringing had a lot to do with it. One of the key ways that SSA can be developed is through the interactions between mother and son. It is thought that in addition to the father being perceived as absent or abusive, the mother also sees the son as a means of emotional support that she does not get from the father.[27]

In my case, I think the model holds true. I don't think that she was consciously aware of it, but she did use me as an emotional crutch. Because of that improper emotional relationship coupled with my father's emotional distance and abuse, I was confused about my own sexuality. When I finally reconnected with my lost masculine essence, I was left to deal with my feelings about women.

So, as I had to forgive my father, I now had to forgive my mother. This was quite difficult for me for a number of reasons. First, I always saw my father as the aggressor and always preferred my mother to him, so it was hard to make that switch. In the whole scheme of things, she had caused me less direct harm than he did, so I never even really saw her part in the formation of my SSA and thus did not see a need to address or forgive her.

---

[27]   See Joseph Nicolosi, *Reparative Therapy of Male Homosexuality: A New Clinical Approach* (Lanham, MD: Rowman & Littlefield Publishers, 2004), particularly chapters 4–10 and Gerard J. M. Van Den Aardweg, *The Battle for Normality: A Guide for (Self-) Therapy for Homosexuality* (San Francisco, CA: Ignatius Press), chapters 1–4.

In reality, though, she *did* have her part.

Her biggest failing with regard to me, besides using me to fill her own emotional needs, was in not *defending* me from my father.

She *allowed* him to abuse me.

Yes, she did comfort me when it happened and, yes, she did address the issue with him, but after having children of my own, I realize that if anyone (including my wife) ever consistently harmed my children, I would take them out of harm's way. No question.

I would do it.

My wife would do it.

I can't believe that my mother *didn't* do it.

Given her own background and her own issues, I can understand why she didn't, but the point is still that she left me in harm's way and her inaction on this matter served to solidify my own problems.

After Judith and I were married, I needed to break that emotional bond with my mother. In the book of Genesis, we read:

> So the LORD God caused a deep sleep to fall upon the man, and while he slept took one of his ribs and closed up its place with flesh; and the rib which the LORD God had taken from the man he made into a woman and brought her to the man. Then the man said,
>
> > "This at last is bone of my bones
> > > and flesh of my flesh;
> > she shall be called Woman,
> > > because she was taken out of Man."

Therefore a man leaves his father and his mother
and cleaves to his wife, and they become one flesh.
(2:21–25)

Once I started down my journey of healing, I gradually
began to sever the parts of that emotional bond which were
not healthy, but it wasn't until I actually got married that I
completed the process.

Most of this is probably what is considered to be the "normal" breaking of the maternal bond, but for me, it just happened a lot later. When we are infants, the first person we
bond with is (hopefully) our mother, so it stands to reason
that this is one of the strongest bonds we have and truly
we never do lose that bond completely, but particularly for
men, there comes a time when we need a healthy rupture
from it so that we can be transformed into the men God
called us to be.

Men who are better formed in their masculine identities
than I was tend to do this earlier on, perhaps when they are
in high school or college. Some men never manage to break
this bond even long after they are married. Thus, the mother
and daughter-in-law are often at odds and the man is torn
between his wife's home and his mother's home. So the effect
is that he doesn't serve either of them with his full heart.

To help with this task, I actually needed the support and
encouragement of my wife who would very gently point out
to me all the areas where I had not yet grown into my full
masculinity. With her help, I was able to see the areas I still
needed to address, and over many years, I eventually did.

Besides my mother, I also needed to come to terms with the fact that most of the women in my family, with exception of my grandmother, (although good people whom I love dearly) were not particularly warm and nurturing, at least not in the way *I* needed.

That being said, I don't really see them as all that different from most women in society; they might actually even be a little bit better, but the one thing I can correctly point out, I think, is that they did not strive for Christ-centered holiness, at least not then.

The Second Vatican Council called all Christians, not just the ordained ministers, to holiness and it is this very holiness which makes the Church.

> Thus it is evident to everyone, that all the faithful of Christ of whatever rank or status, are called to the fullness of the Christian life and to the perfection of charity; by this holiness as such a more human manner of living is promoted in this earthly society. In order that the faithful may reach this perfection, they must use their strength accordingly as they have received it, as a gift from Christ. They must follow in His footsteps and conform themselves to His image seeking the will of the Father in all things. They must devote themselves with all their being to the glory of God and the service of their neighbor. In this way, the holiness of the People of God will grow into an abundant harvest of good, as is admirably shown by the life of so many saints in Church history.[28]

---

[28]   Paul VI, *Dogmatic Constitution on the Church: Lumen Gentium,*

It is our duty to always strive for this holiness, though we will, at times, fall short.

We owe this to ourselves.

We owe this to society.

We owe this to our families.

We owe this to our *children*.

We owe this to Our Lord and Savior, Jesus Christ.

November 21, 1964, http://www.vatican.va/archive/hist_councils/ ii_vatican_council/documents/vat-ii_cons_19651207_gaudium-et-spes_en.html, no. 40.

"Honor Your Father"

Earlier in the book, I detailed my relationship with my dad growing up and showed how one of the "results" of that relationship was the development of my homosexual orientation. To be sure, my father definitely committed sins against me. He eventually realized it too.

One day before I was married, we were alone in the kitchen and he said to me, "You know, I didn't always do right by you when you were growing up. I'm not proud of everything I've done. There's no such thing as a perfect father."

That much was true, at least on this side of heaven. My response to this was not something I would have expected to say. Based on what I remember of the conversation, I definitely got the impression that he was asking for my forgiveness, although he didn't put it in those exact words.

Although what he said was true and he had hurt me a lot growing up, I also knew, in retrospect, that I had my part in my development as well. I had my own sins to confess. I had sinned against him as well. There is really no point in comparing his sin to mine because in the end, all sin ends in death unless it is repented of and stopped.

Well aware of my own sinfulness in our relationship, I simply stated, "There's no such thing as a perfect son either."

I think this exchange of forgiveness soothed both of our hearts and allowed us to move on together. Although we never had the ideal father-son relationship, before he died, we accepted each other for who we were and I can say that our relationship, while not without conflict, was definitely *peaceful.*

I also am very mindful of the fact that just as I had to separate from my mother psychologically after I was married, I also had to do this with my father. It actually happened between the births of my second and third children.

Although Dad and I had a meeting of the minds well before I got married, after the birth of my son, there was a day in which I needed to push the limits of that relationship as well. Now, anyone who knew my dad would say that he could be stubborn and controlling. He admitted the same thing himself.

One day he came over for some reason that I honestly do not remember at this point. He began pressing me about some matter, the importance of which has since waned. The point, however, is that I finally pushed back, not physically, but emotionally and aired a lot of the grievances I had with how he and my mother sometimes treated me.

It grew to a very heated exchange with lots of yelling, but the ultimate result was that Dad realized that I had come into my own manhood and although he might not always agree with my decisions or choices on certain things, he basically allowed me to do things my own way from that day forward and our relationship has been an adult one ever since. It wasn't pleasant, but it had to be done and it definitely changed our relationship for the better. Before he died, he even sometimes confided in me, and unlike the past, I did not simply take Mom's side against him but tried to listen and understand instead.

That being said, there is a definite reason that God commanded that we honor our parents. "Children, obey your parents in the Lord, for this is right. 'Honor your father and mother' (this is the first commandment with a promise), 'that it may be well with you and that you may live long on the earth.' Fathers, do not provoke your children to anger, but bring them up in the discipline and instruction of the Lord" (Eph 6:1–4).

Saint Paul notes in the referenced quotation, that it is the only commandment in the "big ten" which has attached to it a specific earthly blessing. God knows that obedience is not easy for those of us without Mary and Joseph for parents! We are fallen creatures, and so are our parents. I think that's why he offers that tangible blessing of a "long life" to those who do it.

Now when we say "honor" our parents, Christ does not require of us a slavish obedience, particularly when what our parents want us to do might not be the healthiest thing for us, but he does command respect in their regard, and that is where I "missed the mark" growing up.

It is all very understandable. My father was someone who caused me harm, an aggressor against whom I had to defend myself. It is only natural that I would defend myself in the only way a child could—through rebelliousness, against him and any man in authority whom I felt did not respect me (regardless of objective reality).

With Dad, I said and did a lot of things I shouldn't have when I was still under his roof. Once I became old enough that he was not a physical threat to me anymore, I did things to deliberately provoke him. I did whatever I could to put him down in any way I could as often as I could. I tried to make him look *stupid*.

I tried to make myself appear better than he was in the ways that I knew I surpassed him. I disobeyed him whenever possible and constantly tried to manipulate and undercut his legitimate authority. I was openly defiant and disrespectful. For these and all my sins against him, I am heartily sorry.

That's the terrible thing about sin. It is never truly private and it hurts not only the person being sinned against but also the sinner and more indirectly the Church and even more broadly, the whole community. For me, this resulted not only in an even more strained relationship with Dad but with other men in my life, even those that might have been in a position to fill that need that my father couldn't.

To start with, I always respected men in authority who I felt knew what they were talking about, such as male teachers and priests, and I don't ever recall being openly disrespectful of any male superior, but I do think that some of my issues with Dad spilled onto my relationship with men in coaching positions.

This probably stemmed from the fact that I had such a disconnect with the sports world—an area in which Dad clearly surpassed me. I ran both track and cross-country in high school, and truth be told, our coaches were pretty good. They always taught good morals, were not verbally or physically abusive, and generally were pretty nice guys. Although winning was important, it was not everything to them, but they never shied away from pushing us and challenging us.

They would constantly tell us that the sport of running was less about physical ability and more about practice, commitment, and drive. They often said that running well was only 10 percent physical but 90 percent mental. As with other sports, I wasn't very good at running.

By the grace of God, I managed to earn a letter in cross-country one season, but never in track, despite having run for four years. I must have looked like such a loser to them, but they still let me stay on the team, constantly trying to get me to improve.

My problem was that I never really listened to them or their advice. I mean, I heard what they said and gave them lip-service, but never really did what they said to do. I somehow thought that their expertise didn't apply to me and that I was just "bad" at it. I focused on what I considered their "bad" aspects and concluded that they were heartless jerks like the rest of the men and they just didn't understand me.

So, what happened? The self-fulfilling prophecy.

I never really improved and I discounted what these men said simply because they were sports-minded men like Dad.

Now, in my Christian walk in talking with other men, I realize that a lot of men do not have great relationships with their fathers. It seems to be more the rule then the exception, and this is really a shame.

Our duty as men is to always reflect the fatherhood of God and the power of Jesus Christ to everyone we meet, especially our own families. Knowing my own story and that of others makes me see just how deep a wound the devil has inflicted on the Church by attacking masculinity.

We have a lot of work to do.

"Everyone Who Commits
Sin Is a Slave of Sin"

A few years ago, I went out to dinner with Owen. After we finished, we decided to take a stroll around the shopping center. We passed by the window of a national chain restaurant known mostly for its well-endowed, scantily clad waitresses but apparently "the wings are also very good."

Owen said to me, "I have to avert my eyes. That is just going to incite lust in me. Don't you have that problem?"

I responded, half-jokingly, "Dude, you know I like *men*!"

He wryly retorted, "I don't get *that* at all!"

We both laughed as we left the view of the restaurant.

Although I tried to infuse some humor into an uncomfortable situation, the truth is that our conversation really made me think.

As I mentioned before, in the midst of my struggle with same-sex attraction, I really desired sexual contact with other men. I was lusting after other men to get what I thought I was missing in my own masculinity. Through my own healing journey, I learned a lot about masculinity and its development.

To begin with, a poor grasp of a man's own masculine identity is not the sole problem of men who struggle with

SSA. It can manifest itself in a variety of ways with different men, not all of which involve lusting after other men. In some men, it surfaces as same-sex attractions, for others it is an addiction to heterosexual pornography, masturbation, adultery, promiscuous sex, pedophilia, gender disorders, or combinations of all of them.

If we act on any of the above, these acts are sins against life and all of them ultimately enslave us. Fortunately, most men do not have to deal with homosexuality directly, or if they do, it is just a passing phase or some "confusion" during their adolescent years, which more or less resolves itself as the boy grows.

I need to emphasize a really important point here. The problem of boys lacking sufficient masculine identity is a widespread one.

It is very tempting for men to say, "Well, I'm not that bad. At least I'm not *gay!*"

However, just because a man does not suffer from attractions to other men does not mean that he has a healthy sense of the masculine, as my conversation with Owen demonstrated. The fortunate thing is that we both have a healthy understanding of our sexuality. Although we don't struggle in the same way, we can see our respective warped views of sex and of other people as deficits in our own masculinity.

Specifically, in my case, I was largely healed of my lust for men, but now a lot of people ask me, "Do you lust after women now?"

The answer is (usually) no because in healing SSA, I am not trying to replace one form of lust with another. So true healing of my lust for men is not accomplished by replacing it with a lust for women.

In the course of healing, many SSA men will often try heterosexual porn in hopes that they will enjoy looking at naked women and therefore accelerate the healing process. In reality though, for many this tends to lead to even more confusion because the man is still committing a sinful act.

The unfortunate thing in our society is that promiscuity in men is praised, and if a man goes out and boasts of his many "conquests" of women, he is admired and called a "player" or "stud" or even in some cases, a "real" man. I'm sure every one of us knows of that "macho" man who struts around and tries to have sex with as many women as possible.

Maybe you are that man.

Mortal sin is mortal sin and it all leads to only one place.

That man is as much in danger of losing his immortal soul as the man who has sex with other men.

I have news for you, brothers. If your sense of self is governed by how many women you conquer, you are not a *real* man. You are not even free. You are a slave and only Jesus Christ can bring you freedom.

Christ says in John's Gospel, "Truly, truly, I say to you, everyone who commits sin is a slave of sin" (8:34).

While the man with SSA uses other men to try and "steal" their masculinity to supplement what he perceives as lacking in his own, the man with what I call hyper-heterosexual desires steals his sense of masculinity from women. At some level, the man doesn't feel that he's "man enough." He consistently tries to prove his own manhood to himself by having sex with as many women as possible.

In both cases, men are taking the incredible God-given and God-ordained gift of sexuality and stealing it from the other partner. It doesn't mitigate the sin if the act is consensual. The only difference is that the two parties have agreed to steal each other's sexuality. Only a marriage covenant blessed by God is, as the Church teaches, the "remedy" for this.

Pornography and masturbation are similar and also incredibly widespread problems with men. While it is true that in these instances, the man is not sinning directly with another person, it is also just as harmful. With one, the man is stealing and degrading in his own heart another person's body while with the other, he is using the gift of his sexuality to satisfy only himself, instead of the one for whom that gift is reserved. In the old days, this used to be called "self-abuse."

Although we generally call it by its scientific term now, it really *is* sexual abuse of one's self, and this is why it can never really be truly satisfying outside the marital embrace; it always leaves one empty and wanting for more.

God intended that sex be "addicting," properly understood; it is what draws the man to his wife, and quite literally, "makes the two become one flesh." A man cannot physically or spiritually unite his genitals with another man, or a pornographic image, or a fantasy, or with his own body; therefore, he constantly seeks more and more. While a happily married man's sex drive might not (and should not) diminish except for biological reasons, the sexual act serves a unitive function for the couple. This is why it is often called "a remedy for concupiscence."

Two men simply cannot become one flesh. God didn't design us that way, and any biological argument to the contrary is untenable.

"You Shall Not Make for Yourself a Graven Image"

Many years ago, a friend let me borrow his copy of a film called *Fight Club*, which was based on a book of the same name by author Chuck Palahniuk. I did not really know what to expect when I watched the film except what could be obviously gleaned from the title, that it was violent. Since it was such a cult classic, I decided to sit down and see why. What followed, despite its violence and gratuitous sex scenes (thus, I can't unreservedly recommend it), was a film that really hit on the essential core of my masculine being.

In a nutshell, the story is about a fictional narrator with no name who has become disaffected with himself and his life. He then meets this bold, non-conformist rebel named Tyler Durden. Tyler is everything that today's American man would want to be. Played by Brad Pitt in the film, he is bold, muscular, good-looking, and great in bed.

He also appeals to the "wild" side of the narrator (and the viewer?), who begins to take on some of Tyler's characteristics as his own. One of the things Tyler introduces the narrator to is an underground "fight club" where men fight, bare-knuckled and bare-chested. It is from these fights that the men regain a sense of the masculinity that life in modern America has stolen from them.

Although he enjoys this foray into his more primitive self, the narrator begins to have doubts about the whole thing, particularly when Tyler has the men start committing violent crimes. This starts a love-hate relationship between the main character and Tyler, who leads the narrator into all sorts of situations where he grapples with what it means to be a man. The climax of the film is when the narrator finally confronts Tyler and learns (spoiler alert!) that Tyler is really a part of him, an alter-ego.

This is the part of the movie that really struck a chord for me because I had my own version of Tyler Durden. Now, "my" Tyler didn't get me into all the trouble of the one in the movie, nor was he ever anything other than a creation of my own mind, but he did stunt my growth as a man and he did set up expectations of masculinity for me that I could not fulfill, which weakened what little masculine identity I had.

"My" Tyler was born out of my own body image issues. Because of the physical abuse I suffered when I was younger, I thought that the way to make myself safe was to wait until I was bigger than my father. Thus, I imagined the man I would "grow up to be." This man would be tall and muscular with long blond hair and would have the admiration of the room whenever he walked in. At some level, I think I realized that what I had constructed was an idol that I had created to replace the man God had created me to be in clear violation of his command in Exodus 20:1–6:

And God spoke all these words, saying,

"I am the LORD your God, who brought you out of the land of Egypt, out of the house of bondage.

"You shall have no other gods before me.

"You shall not make for yourself a graven image, or any likeness of anything that is in heaven above, or that is in the earth beneath, or that is in the water under the earth; you shall not bow down to them or serve them; for I the LORD your God am a jealous God."

My idolatrous version of myself was not the man God had created but rather the one I thought God *should* have created. I clung to this idol through my teenage and college years. When it became obvious that I was not going to grow any more and that I had a rather thin frame, I still clung to that idol. It wasn't until after my experience at Fatima that the Lord told me clearly that this "Tyler" was an idol standing in opposition to him and to the real man he knew was inside me—the one he made.

It was so hard and so painful for me to let him go. I can't say that killing "my" Tyler happened instantly, but over time, whenever I would engage in the fantasy of the man I should be, I offered that image to Jesus, and he always took it. One day, it just never came back.

Even though I was rid of the idol, I still struggled with body image issues. I always thought I was too small and not stereotypically masculine enough. Objectively, I'm not a big guy at all; I'm only 5′7″ and around 150 pounds. Whenever I come across a guy who's well-built and tall or who just has a very masculine presence, I still sometimes feel insecure about myself, despite knowing that I shouldn't and that to do so is wrong.

To compensate for these feelings, I used to lift weights regularly. It helped. I liked the feeling of being strong and I liked the way people looked at me when I was jacked. I could be completely clothed, but people still noticed. I got a real sense of confidence from it, so I enjoyed doing it. That was the good side of it.

The bad side is that I started to put my identity in my strength and muscularity. In other words, lifting became a kind of "fix" for my own insecurity. Rather than deal with my feelings of inadequacy, I tried to cover them in muscle.

I'm not saying that working out is a bad thing to do; it definitely helped me to feel more masculine, but it didn't really help me get at the root of the problem of my own weak identity.

So God repeatedly reminded me of this by allowing small injuries that prevented me from lifting weights from time to time. One year, as Lent was about to begin, I injured my neck. It was taking a really long time to recover, and I was unable to lift.

About ten days into Lent, I was praying in the shower and I heard the Lord clearly say, "I want you to give up lifting weights for forty days."

My immediate and uncensored reaction was, "No! I won't do that!"

I actually began to cry there in the shower. I wanted to lift that bad.

Once I collected myself, I realized that this was an area of myself that I had not fully surrendered to the Lord, so I knew it was for my own good, but it was still a really hard Lent. I was glad when it was over, and by the time Easter rolled around, my neck had healed.

It turned out that it would be almost another year before I could lift again because we ended up moving into a new house unexpectedly and the birth of my first daughter followed immediately thereafter.

It was during this move that the Lord showed me my own masculine essence. Even though it was only across town, the move ended up taking about twelve hours to complete. It was a very long day. Along with my nine-months-pregnant wife (talk about strength!) and six friends, I worked the whole time to move things in and get things settled.

Obviously, everyone was pretty tired at the end of the day. I really didn't think much of it until two weeks later when the baby was born. After I had emailed my household brothers through our group list a picture of me holding my newborn baby girl, I was kind of surprised at a couple of things.

First, several of my household brothers emailed me to tell me how masculine I looked in the picture. They were right. There was something very masculine about that photo even though I was not muscular but actually on the thin side.

One of them, who had actually helped me move, posted one of the most incredible affirmations I have ever gotten from another man. There's no way I can possibly do it justice, so I have reprinted it here in its entirety (with very minor edits). This is what he posted to the entire group about me:

> He is a deceivingly strong dude with both physical strength and endurance (We moved heavy stuff for

> like, 12 hours or something crazy. We were the only
> ones left standing). He has that certain quality about
> him . . . that quality that you can only get from your-
> self and then from God. That quality that one gets
> when he's met his own weakness and brokenness and
> wrestles and fights and struggles and cries . . . but then
> accepts and loves (himself) and therefore conquers
> and stands in peace! Truly, he has been through the
> trial, it's all over him! I hardly know him as I know
> some of you all, but his fasting and prayers helped save
> my butt. He's earned my respect.

That email resonated with something inside of me. Although I sometimes have difficulty accepting it, I know it's true.

Despite knowing in my head that the Father is pleased with the masculinity he gave me, I still continued to struggle in that area.

So, of course, I ended up getting injured again; this time it was my shoulder. This is ironic because it is the one muscle group I seem unable to build up and broad shoulders are one thing with which I was not blessed.

The first few days of the injury were hard to deal with. Whenever I saw big or strong-looking men, I was really hard on myself and it seemed like I had to go through the detachment process all over again. It happened once or twice again, but I think I finally got the point.

What the Lord taught me through all this is that sin is at the heart of my insecurity. It took me quite a while to figure out exactly what this sin was. According to the explanation of 1 John 2:16 in the *Catechism of the Catholic Church*, there are three types of lust: lust of the flesh, lust of the eyes, and pride of life.

> St. John distinguishes three kinds of covetousness or concupiscence: lust of the flesh, lust of the eyes, and pride of life. In the Catholic catechetical tradition, the ninth commandment forbids carnal concupiscence; the tenth forbids coveting another's goods.
>
> Etymologically, "concupiscence" can refer to any intense form of human desire. Christian theology has given it a particular meaning: the movement of the sensitive appetite contrary to the operation of the human reason. The apostle St. Paul identifies it with the rebellion of the "flesh" against the "spirit." Concupiscence stems from the disobedience of the first sin. It unsettles man's moral faculties and, without being in itself an offense, inclines man to commit sins.[29]

Leaving the first aside, I would like to focus on the second and third types.

There were two biblical verses that helped me to come to grips with this pattern of sin in my life. The first is from Exodus 20:17, which reads, "You shall not covet your neighbor's house; you shall not covet your neighbor's wife, or his manservant, or his maidservant, or his ox, or his ass, or anything that is your neighbor's." The other is the aforementioned warning about lust of the heart in Matthew 5:28.

---

[29] *Catechism of the Catholic Church,* 2nd. ed. (Washington, DC: United States Catholic Conference, 2000), nos. 2514–15.

At first, I didn't see the differentiation nor the integral connection between these three types of lust. I thought that "lust of the eyes" meant lusting in the heart. That is seeing a desirable person and lusting after him or her even without acting on those lustful feelings.

In actuality though, this is still a manifestation of carnal lust (of the flesh). The truth is that that if we lust only in our hearts, we have already committed the very act that we were lusting about.

Thus, lust of the eyes has to be something a bit different. When I researched exactly what was meant by that, the equivalent word is *covetousness*. What exactly does it mean to covet? Most sources define it as an inordinate desire for something or someone. It is often equated with greed and jealousy and, most of all, *envy*.

Basically, it is when someone desperately wants an object of the desire so much that they "lust" after it much the same way someone would lust after someone else sexually. Some translators argue that the original Hebrew word translated as *covet* is actually a much stronger word that is more analogous to the word *take*.

So this is not just a simple matter of admiring something and thinking that you would like to have the object or something similar. For example, I may desire that piece of chocolate cake, so I eat it. In most cases, there is nothing sinful in that.

Envious lust of the eyes goes deeper than that. For me, it is the key root of many of my sins. After my healing, it would really bother me that I would still find some men so sexually attractive. When I really took it to prayer, I found that in my heart of hearts, I didn't really want sex with them, but rather, I desired them for their masculinity. I wanted to *take* and possess their masculinity as my own. I *lusted* for their masculinity.

So, in other words, I was coveting their masculinity or their masculine features that I perceived to be lacking in myself. So, yeah, I was literally coveting another man's ass (or shoulders or arms or chest or size).

All joking aside though, I noticed that when I found myself doing this, if I took it to prayer, I would see that I had an inordinate, unhealthy, and sinful desire for the gifts God gave to other men.

This was really the key to understanding my same-sex attraction, at least from the perspective of my body image. I wanted what I could not have, so I would lift weights to try and get that, and when it didn't work out (again, pardon the bad pun), I would become discouraged and start envying what other men had.

Once I realized this, I constantly gave these covetous desires over to the Lordship of Christ and confessed my sins to him directly and also through the sacrament of Reconciliation.

I can remember one time in particular when I was really struggling with the pain of my SSA and without even thinking, I said to myself, "This would be so much easier if I just had sex with a guy!"

It's true. At least in the short-run, I could have gotten my "fix" through sex, but I knew that in the longer term, it would not really fix the issues within me that needed fixing. If I had sex with a man to whom I was attracted, I would have probably felt better in the moment but then been left with a nagging insecurity that I'm not *him*. I don't have the features I desired in him.

What I needed to do was accept and love myself for the man God made me, not any idol I had constructed and not some other man whose characteristics seemed to fulfill my own thoughts of true masculinity.

Just me.

Just the way God made me, faults and imperfections and all. I needed to accept myself as *the man God made me to be*, not the one I thought *he should have made me* to be. This was the idol of envy and covetousness in my heart that I had to smash.

Like the character in the book and film, I came to realize that "my" Tyler was really representative of my own God-given masculinity, and although I will never have his physical appearance, I now know that I am strong because it is Christ who strengthens me.

It is just as Saint Paul says in the Letter to Romans, "We know that our old self was crucified with him, so that our sinful body might be done away with, that we might no longer be enslaved to sin" (6:6).

My "old self" was "my" Tyler.

The Lord himself crucified him so that I could be free.

"The Rain Is Over and Gone"

So, after nearly ten years had gone by, I began to feel stirrings in my heart to share my story more publicly than I had in the past. Although I shared my testimony in limited "as-needed" circumstances, I had never really felt the call to share more widely.

That was about to change.

As I mentioned earlier, I am a high school English teacher at a public school. In the public school, particularly in the "progressive" community where I work, it is often not possible to openly share the Gospel of Jesus Christ with students (or even coworkers) on school grounds except in very limited circumstances. When I last counted, there were less than a dozen openly believing Christians in a staff of nearly three hundred.

Of course, many more people than that attend church (even Catholic churches) and talk about the more superficial aspects of faith, but few would be willing to actually pray with me or share on deeper levels of spirituality.

Thus, I find myself needing to live the Gospel as best as I possibly can, and invariably some people will ask about my spiritual life and then I am in a better position to talk about what the Lord has done for me. Don't get me wrong. I never hide who I am, I just try to use prudence and not to come across as "preachy." Also, I always try to let my Christian faith and Catholic morality govern what I teach and how I teach to the greatest extent possible.

I often refer to it as working in "Caesar's house" and am mindful of "rendering unto Caesar" that which is his. Most of my work life fits Caesar's domain and I have accepted that, but ultimately, by virtue of my baptismal vows, I am a part of Christ's Mystical Body in the world and all of my actions either build the Body or break it down, because "the things that are God's" (Mt 22:21) are always more important than those that belong to Caesar.

In the early Church, Christians began infiltrating all the areas of Roman life and some of them actually worked for the emperor himself. Obviously, these people would have needed to have a "hidden spirituality" in order to not arouse suspicion. Of course, it was just this "hidden spirituality" which eventually proved to be the proverbial "yeast" that leavened the whole empire.

So, although I have openly shared my faith on numerous occasions at work, sometimes the Father has work for me which has required that I share more deeply, and I have always tried to be docile to that call.

One such time came upon me very unexpectedly. After I had been married for about two years, I received a phone call at my work voicemail from the youth minister of the local Catholic church in town, who had seen our wedding picture in Franciscan University's alumni magazine along with a blurb which noted the district for which I taught.

He reached out in hopes of connecting with a fellow alum. After we had gotten to know each other a bit better, one day he called me and asked me to be a part of his youth group's retreat team. Ordinarily, this would have posed no problem. I had served on several retreat teams before and was well acquainted with format and logistics.

This retreat would be different.

I had no idea just how different it would be nor how greatly God was going to bless me.

The reason I was so hesitant was that this retreat would serve the teens of the town where I worked, possibly even the students with whom I worked with directly.

This posed a real dilemma for me since I know how rumors start on baseless banter and I wasn't sure I wanted to put myself out there like that. That was the first obstacle, and although I was uncomfortable, I still agreed to do it, placing my trust in the power of Jesus Christ.

Now, the retreat followed a specific format that required the retreat team to meet together for a matter of months to discern the Lord's call about the specific way that each team member would serve the retreatants. The beginning of this process is that all of the team members share their life stories and how God has worked in their lives in order to get them to the place they are now.

When it came to be my turn, I wasn't so sure how much I wanted to share about my past struggles. I could obviously have shared my story and left out some of the details under the heading of "sexual struggles." I wasn't so sure that the Lord was going to be satisfied with just that this time. Again, because this is the town where I work, I was hesitant to share because these were some of the parents of my students and members of the community. But never far from my mind was that promise I had made to Our Lady in Portugal.

So I discussed it and prayed about it with Judith, and she told me that she was fine with my sharing if I felt the Lord calling me to do so. I really hadn't made up my mind what I was going to do until the night of the meeting, so I sort of "white-knuckled" it. If I chose to share my story at that point, it would have been the first time I was really opening up to a group in public.

No pressure.

As you can probably guess, I did share my story that night, and as you can probably guess again, everyone was extremely supportive. I was amazed at how little people knew about homosexuality and its origins. The team asked me lots of questions and told me that my story had changed the way they viewed homosexuality.

It was from sharing this that I began to see that there is a real need to get this truth out there, not just to Catholics and other Christians who might struggle with these issues, but also for the Church at large, which, unfortunately, is very poorly formed, for the most part, at this point in history. I know that I made an impact that night, and although it was a small one, I knew those folks would remember my story if the issue of homosexuality ever entered their lives again.

After that night, the other retreat members shared their stories and our discernment continued. Personally, I was really struggling with how much of my story to share with the teenagers. By its nature, the retreat required personal witnesses, and the team had discerned that I would be presenting the Saturday night talk, which was themed around the Holy Eucharist. As anyone who has been on retreat before knows, Saturday night is the "power" night—the talk that "makes" the retreat. In other words, it's meant to be the climax of the weekend, so it *had* to be good.

Even after my arrival to the retreat center, I really struggled down in the depths of my soul as to whether or not I should share it. My main problem besides the potential that these kids might be or eventually become my students was also that even though there is supposed to be confidentiality, everyone knows that with most teens, there is no such thing.

Thus, I was almost guaranteed that word of this would get out to the school at large in some fashion, to both students and staff. Complicating matters was that at the time, the principal of the school was openly gay and most of the teachers (some of whom also identified themselves as gay) would probably profess "alternative lifestyles" as perfectly acceptable. In my mind, I was opening the door to persecution, and quite honestly, I was afraid.

I brought these struggles before the Lord and basically argued the merits of it in prayer. Here is an encapsulated (and much polished) version of our daylong prayer conversation.

The Lord: "I have called you to speak the truth without fear."

Me: "But these are my students and the people I work with."

The Lord: "Am I not more important?"

Me: "Satan could twist what I say and use it against me."

The Lord: "Who do you think is more powerful, then? Satan is under my power and anything he does is done with my permission."

Me: "But the principal is openly gay!"

The Lord: "If he is not ashamed to say what he thinks, why are you ashamed to say what I want you to say and to testify to what I have done for you? If he has the freedom to speak, why don't you?"

He got me on the last one. I had no argument there.

At that moment I knew what I would be speaking about that night. It was not without consolation, however. As I continued my prayer, I really began to feel scared about what I was about to do and I began to lose confidence in myself. Did God really heal me? Am I really all that changed? Might not at least a part of this be in my head?

As I pondered all of these questions, a Scripture came to mind from the Song of Solomon. If you have not ever read that book of the Bible, it is basically erotic metaphoric love poetry in which God is the lover come to ravish and fulfill the soul of the believer.

The soul, even the soul of a man, is always seen as feminine in that it is always the receiver of God's love first, before it can give that love away. Thus, the first lines comprised the love song that God sang to my soul.

> My beloved speaks and says to me:
> "Arise, my love, my fair one,
>   and come away;
> for lo, the winter is past,
>   the rain is over and gone. (Sg 2:10–11)

It was his way of telling me that my struggle in this area was indeed past, not that I still wouldn't have issues with masculine identity, but that my sexuality had truly been made whole in this area and I need not fear it ever again.

As the tears welled up in my eyes, I felt an abiding sense of peace which grew as the day went on.

The Lord even began to provide the logistics of the talk for me. Up until that time, I wasn't even sure how I would present. In addition to the talk, I also had to choose a song that would go with the theme of the talk.

Going into the retreat, I had nothing. No song and only a vague idea of how to present it.

The only preparation I had done was to formulate the points of my witness that I wanted to be sure I covered. I tried to come up with a song, all to no avail. It wasn't until I arrived that the Lord provided the song—the *perfect* song—one that let me know how much he loved me and wanted me to share my experience with those teens that weekend.

"We Have Seen His Star"

Although December 25 is the day set aside by the universal Church (at least in the West) to celebrate Christmas, many might not be aware of why that date was chosen. One thing that many biblical historians argue is that Christmas probably did not occur in the middle of winter, based on biblical evidence. Others disagree.

Pope Benedict XVI, for instance, in his wonderful book *The Blessing of Christmas*, notes that the earliest written record of it states that Jesus was born on December 25 during Chanukah, the great Festival of Lights. How fitting that the Lord who would "suddenly enter His temple" would be born during the feast commemorating its restoration.[30]

So there are a lot of reasons why the Church decided to celebrate Christmas at this time of year. One of the most beautiful is that the Winter Solstice, a pagan festival, was held on the first day of winter, which, of course, is the darkest night of the year. The Church thought it most fitting that the darkest night of the year should be the time that Christians would celebrate the rising of the Light of the World, because it would be on that "night divine" that the light would shine its brightest.

---

[30]   Joseph Cardinal Ratzinger, *The Blessing of Christmas* (San Francisco, CA: Ignatius Press, 2007), 105–9.

Even during my darkest of times, Christmas was always a time of great joy and hopeful expectation for me. Any God who would become a little child was really worthy of praise and adoration.

Even today, Christmas is my favorite time of year. I love the decorations, the lights, the songs, the food, the liturgies, just everything about it. It is the night when the whole world seems wrapped in a mantle of joy and the presence of the Holy Spirit is palpable, as if God's heaven were opening and shining its own radiance down to the earth for just one brief moment in time.

It should have not surprised me then that God would have chosen for me to approach my talk through a theme of such great joy. As I mentioned before, I had no idea what song to use when I arrived, but as the team arrived to set up for the retreat, I happened to see a CD collection that one of the team members brought to use over the course of the weekend. In it, I saw a Christmas CD by Christian artist Twila Paris. Immediately, one of the songs came to my mind, the one called "Wandering Pilgrim," a song about following the star to find Jesus.

There it was in a song I had heard a hundred times over many Christmases; it was my life story—the lyrics were all about *me*. I am the wandering pilgrim who felt so far from home and struggled to seek that Blessed Messiah of Bethlehem. I needed the escort to show me the way. I needed to look to the wonderful star to see that my salvation was upon me. We read in Matthew 2:1–2: "Now when Jesus was born in Bethlehem of Judea in the days of Herod the king, behold, wise men from the East came to Jerusalem, saying, 'Where is he who has been born king of the Jews? For we have seen his star in the East, and have come to worship him.'"

Healing, grace, wholeness, and joy were all mine for the asking if I just followed that wonderful star.

I followed that star. I followed *her*.

The star, as the Church proclaims in her liturgy, is none other than the Blessed Virgin. She, along with Christ, is acclaimed as the "morning star," as the herald of a new day. She is also venerated as *stella maris*, the "star of the sea" who leads sailors home across the dark and treacherous ocean waters. I followed her and it led me to her Divine Son, Jesus Christ. It all made sense now. On this cold weekend in January, it was all so clear, as clear as a starry night.

Now, for the first time, I was to tell a whole group of people about Christ's wonderful star. No longer was I the lost pilgrim seeking his face, but now I was to help others see that star and begin following it . . . to the cradle . . . and the cross . . . and the resurrection.

As my mission solidified, I began to experience a profound sense of the Holy Spirit within me as I had never experienced before. It started off as a feeling of joy and peace and then it continued to grow and grow as my prayer intensified during the day.

In the evening before the talk there was an opportunity for the whole team to go to confession. The chapel was an old gothic structure with monastery seating, meaning that two sets of pews (and their occupants) faced each other, with the altar and sanctuary more or less in the center of the pews.

I happened to be sitting across from most of the retreat team. As I sat down, I can only say that I felt radiant with

God's love. Radiance is the only word I can use to describe
it. I could feel his very power and glory coursing through my
body and shining through me. When I came out of the confessional, I sat back down in my pew basking in God's love.
I closed my eyes and tried to savor this deep communion as
much as I could, for these "mountaintop" experiences never
last long outside of eternity. I thought that this was a subjective prayer experience meant only as a consolation for me.

However, when I opened my eyes, I was shocked to look
into the faces of the retreat team sitting across from me as
tears streamed down their faces. It was not subjective at all.
They saw it too! They stared at me as the tears continued to
roll down their faces.

Like that bright star of the sea, for this one brief moment,
my soul also "magnified" the Lord and my spirit exulted in
God my savior, for he had indeed done great things for me
and holy, indeed, is his Name.

Finally, the woman who was the retreat coordinator mus-
tered up the wherewithal to say something to me.

She said something to the effect of, "I don't know what
I'm trying to say here, but you look so beautiful and so
peaceful."

No one could really put into words what they saw, but
everyone was visibly affected.

I remained behind in the chapel for some time to continue my prayer, and when I emerged, I felt so powerful,
so bold, and so confident and I was ready to give this talk.
Gone was any sense of fear when I walked out in front of
fifty teenagers to tell them of my life's struggle and what the
Lord had done for me.

I don't really remember much of that night or even of people's reactions to the talk because I don't think that was God's purpose for me. He just wanted me to know that I should, as St. John Paul II exhorted, "Be Not Afraid!"

That talk was the best I have ever given—not because of what I said but because of the power of God's anointing. Although I have given many presentations since then, I never had an experience like that again. It achieved its intended effect as a consolation for me. I do not really know how, and I may never know on this side of the veil, but I helped to advance God's kingdom in some small way that night. I also knew that I was meant to tell my story to anyone who would listen.

I know I need to tell of the glory of Jesus Christ and the power of his holy cross, particularly to men who struggle sexually and seek God's healing because if he can heal my twisted sexuality, he can heal anyone's. We are not the slaves of Satan but the sons of God. I want to show the waiting world his Great Star, who always leads to him.

Our Lady, Star of the Sea, Star of the Messiah, Morning Star and Queen-Mother of the Son of David, *pray for us.*

Pray for me.

"O Lord, You Will Increase Your Gifts in Me"

One question people often ask me is, "How do you know you have really changed? What proof do you have?"

In the course of my healing, there were, as I have mentioned previously, many times when I myself wondered if I had really changed or if what was happening to me was just a product of my own wishful thinking.

Again and again I cling to the knowledge that although I never identified myself with a gay lifestyle, I certainly had deep, abiding, and erotic attraction to men. I wanted to have sexual relationships exclusively with men. I fantasized about it, desired it, and *coveted* it. The only things I didn't do were to publicly identify myself as gay and actually have sex with a man.

This is the truth.

It is equally true that I no longer desire any of these things in my heart of hearts.

I have been healed.

I have been freed by the Son.

Still, the devil knows my area of weakness and attacks me there periodically, even after many years of marriage. One of those times was right before another retreat on which I was serving as a team member. Before the retreat, we all were praying over each other. It was a time when I was going through a lot of temptations to doubt what the Lord had done for me, but it was not something I confessed to anyone, because, the truth be told, I was still fairly confident, but it still bothered me as a nagging thought in the back of my mind that I thought I was just going to have to live with as my proverbial "thorn in the flesh."

Anyway, I took these thoughts to prayer. The team began praying over each other. When it came to be my turn, one of the members of my team prayed over me and got a word from the Lord.

He said, "There is something in your past that you've been healed of. The Lord wants you to know that it is *never* coming back. He wants you to be at peace."

As soon as he said it, I knew the Lord had spoken. It pierced my heart and filled me with a confidence and joy. Since that day, I have never again doubted that the Lord had started a good thing in me and would bring it to its full completion.

As far as actual change in the degree of my own attraction to men, I can also attest to that in several ways. Besides my own knowledge of myself, there a couple of other ways I've been able to verify that this is a true change and not just wishful thinking.

The first is through other people. I know it through people who have known me for a long time noticing the change in me (even those who were never aware of my sexual orientation) and through the close, healthy male friendships which I have kept for well over a decade. I could never sustain

friendships like these before my healing; I was way too insecure and needy. Any friendship I tried to have with a man
simply collapsed under its own weight with few exceptions.

More importantly, I have an incredible marriage and three
wonderful kids. Although not without the difficulties any
marriage goes through, my wife is truly my best friend and
we have an amazing relationship and great sex! Honestly, I
couldn't be happier. When I was twenty, I never dreamed I'd
be where I am today in my forties.

Admittedly, these are both rather subjective measures.
Perhaps the most objective measure of the change within
me is through the content of my dreams. Before my healing,
I would frequently experience erotic and highly sexualized
dreams about men.

St. Augustine of Hippo reported similar problems, albeit
about women. Long after his conversion, he was still bothered by sexual content in his dreams (which of course, are not
sinful, since they are beyond conscious control). Nonetheless, the dreams bothered him. He writes in his *Confessions*:

> But in my memory, of which I have said much, the
> images of things imprinted upon it by my former
> habits still linger on. When I am awake, they obtrude
> themselves upon me, though with little strength. But
> when I dream, they not only give me pleasure but are
> very much like acquiescence in the act. The power
> which these illusory images have over my soul and my
> body is so great that what is no more than a vision can
> influence me in sleep in a way that the reality cannot

do when I am awake. Surely it cannot be that when I
am asleep I am not myself, O Lord my God?[31]

Even long after I was married and had children, I would
often have dreams where I was doing sexual things with men
that I had never even done in reality. Although these dreams
certainly had the potential to upset me, I always tried to
keep them in focus as either the distractions of the devil or
the manifestations of my own needs as a man. I knew that
I had always longed for physical affection from men and
whenever I had one of these dreams, I would bring the sexual content of the dream before the Lord and ask him to
reveal what these dreams symbolized. What I came to realize
is that these dreams were the manifestations of my starved
masculine soul, crying out for its own needs to be met.

The interesting thing about it is that my needs were
already being met. I felt like "one of the guys." I had amazing
friendships. I was respected by men; I was happily married
and happily heterosexual. So then, why these dreams?

Then, the answer came. About ten years into my marriage, the content of the dreams shifted. Now, whenever I
had dreams about men, they were about sharing good times
with them in the dreams. They were now about doing activities together and just enjoying each other. The erotic dreams
had actually changed!

I remember one particularly vivid dream where I was in
a pool with a bunch of naked men who were in the middle of an orgy. The men all stopped what they were doing

---

[31]   Augustine and R. S. Pine-Coffin, *Confessions: Saint Augustine*
       (Penguin Classics, 2015), Book X, chapter 30.

and looked at me. They called to me and tried to entice me to come join them. I actually backed up out of the pool and turned my back on them. It was honestly not even that difficult.

As always, after I have these "new" dreams, I wake up feeling refreshed instead of troubled because I know that I am a man who needs to be loved by men and *is* loved by men. It has even come to the point where I have even refused to do something sexual with a man *in my dreams*! So profound has the Lord's healing transformation been in me!

So what may have started out as distractions from the devil to make me think I was not really healed or to divert me from the path of which the Lord had so firmly planted my feet, instead became affirmations that indeed the Lord had done what he said he would do. I am healed and I am whole. These dreams have now come to symbolize that, and whenever I have one, I wake up rejoicing in gratitude for all the Lord has done for me. His touch has so penetrated me that he has even reached my dark core and brought in his holy light. Interestingly, that is what St. Augustine says would eventually happen to a believer:

> The power of your hand O God Almighty, is indeed great enough to cure all the diseases of my soul. By granting me more abundant grace you can even quench the fire of sensuality which provokes me in my sleep. More and more, O Lord, you will increase your gifts in me so that my soul may follow me to you . . . by your grace it will no longer commit in sleep these shameful, unclean acts inspired by sensual images, . . .

it will not so much as consent to them. . . . For to you
. . . it is no great task to prescribe that no temptations
of this kind . . . should arouse pleasure in me, even in
sleep.[32]

---

[32]   Ibid.

A Man Among Men

So, having gone through all that healing, the big question on your mind is probably, "So, what is life like now?" Have the desires stopped? Have the attractions stopped? The answer I will give is a complicated one. Again, I have to go back to what I said earlier in the book. When I talk about "change," I didn't experience it in terms of something that was there before but is not there now, but rather, I just developed more in my heterosexuality.

I will try to be as specific as possible, but I apologize where I don't do justice to the transformation the Lord has worked. First, I do (and probably always will) have residual effects of homosexuality. Since I used my SSA as a coping mechanism for most of my life, I still have some weak associations and old habits. This is to be completely expected.

From a psychological perspective and according to the principles of classical conditioning, once an association is made in the brain, you can never really undo it completely. This is why so many addicts end up backsliding. This is also why people often need to completely change their lives, avoid places where they committed the sin (and in some cases, even give up former friends and relationships) in order to overcome a particular vice. Of course, different people experience this to different degrees, but it is realistic to expect that at least *some* associations will remain.

In my case, for instance, when I am feeling insecure, my first line of defense is to start dwelling on these attractions. I start wondering about other men. Are they like me? Are they different? Am I different? How? If I find myself attracted to a guy or curious about what he's like, in the past it would have been easy to indulge in fantasy, even if it was not lustful.

After a while, I began to realize that these fantasies were kind of useless to me and were not really what I wanted anyway, so they gradually began to lose their power and became easier and easier to overcome. At this point in time, I still experience attractions to men, but they are of three kinds.

The first kind is an attraction to a man I don't know who I find alluring. He is the type that I just can't pull my eyes away from for some reason. It's not even a lustful thing. There is just something there that I find to be attractive.

More often than not, I find that there are usually two causes to this kind of attraction. The first is that the guy ends up being a really good man, even a Christian. I am thus attracted to his goodness. With this kind of attraction, if it is appropriate, I might try to pursue a friendship with this guy. If not, I just praise God for his goodness and the gift of his masculinity and ask the Lord to bless him.

The second kind is a type of sexual attraction that results not necessarily because I am physically attracted but that the guy has some sort of sexual issue which might not be apparent from the surface. Again, it is a situation where I find myself drawn to the guy but don't know why. It is very similar to how I feel when I see the good guy.

However, with time and discernment, I start to see that it is not really the guy I'm feeling attracted to but rather this guy's sexual sins which also stir up my own lust. Any time we engage in any kind of immoral sexual activity, we invite the demonic to join us. Although sexual sin is not always a path to the demonic and it's certainly not the only one, it is a common one.

These types of guys are the ones I try to steer clear of because of my own past. Oftentimes, I'm not even aware of my own thoughts and feelings during these times. It usually takes a friend or, more often, my wife to help me see through this particular kind of attraction. However, even though this can be a distraction, it is just that.

Despite the fact that I may experience all of these attractions, at their root is really my own insecurity fueled by my own envy and covetousness. Let me give you an example. I recently read an article about a particular actor who is nearly seven feet tall and four hundred pounds of mostly muscle.

As I think most men would be, I was curious as to what this guy looked like, so I looked up some pictures of him online. I have to be honest, he was quite the specimen of masculinity. I greatly admired the sheer size and power of his body. It was not sexual, but the more I looked at him, the more I felt myself unconsciously wishing to be like him, and the more I did that, I started comparing my body to his. Weighing in at only 150 pounds or so, I am probably the size of one of his legs!

Then, it happened.

I started feeling insecure from looking at him. I began to unconsciously tell myself that this guy was a real man, and I began wondering what it would feel like to have his body, to be that *big*! Suddenly, I felt like a little boy again and here was this *man*, in whose league I would never be. I wanted to feel like the man he probably felt like. I wanted his *body*. I wanted to *be* him. Once I realized that my lust of the eyes was making me spiral down into a cyclone of envy which would ultimately end badly for my own masculinity, I stopped myself.

I invited Jesus Christ into my sinful heart and asked him to purify it. With Christ now with me, I forced myself to look at those images of that actor and prayed. First, I thanked God for making me the man he made me, then I thanked him for making the other guy the man he made him. I thanked God for his maleness and my own and asked him to heal my envy and covetousness. By the end of my time, I could see more clearly and that I could not possibly get from this man or from any other what I perceived to be lacking in myself.

Whenever I feel this way, I always confess it to the Lord and ask him to help me understand the nature of these attractions. When I pray it through, I realize that I don't actually want to have sex with men. The thought of it becomes less alluring and more foreign with each passing day. When my physical desires began to abate, for a long time, what remained was a strong feeling to emotionally connect with men. This eventually led to the third type of "attraction": brotherly love.

This is the third kind of attraction, and this is the type that healthy men have for one another. It is the attraction and the desire to be with each other without the erotic element. As I journeyed through my healing, that desire was always interwoven with sexual desire, which I worked through.

Eventually, as I began to grow more and more comfortable in the world of men, the erotic desires gradually faded. I first noticed it with my oldest and closest friends. My love for those guys grew deeper and deeper but the erotic feelings didn't.

One day my former pastor asked me to start a men's ministry with another guy at the parish whom I had never met before. The first time I met him, I was instantly attracted to him. He is good-looking in a rugged, manly way and has a no-nonsense way about him that makes you know that what you see with him is really what you get.

We are on about the most opposite sides of the personality spectrum as you can get. Where I am more cautious, he prefers to jump in more forcefully. But where I prefer to be more "front-and-center," he would rather stay out of the limelight. We definitely do not always see eye-to-eye, nor do we approach ministry the same way, but there is such a complementarity between us that the Lord uses our very different leadership styles as "iron sharpens iron" to effectively run our ministry.

Working with him so closely over the years and needing to resolve so many logistic and pastoral issues together has forged a bond between us with both of us seeing each other at our best and our worst. We have shared our failings and weaknesses and still been there to support each other and build each other in our brotherhood.

One particular incident in the ministry required a lot of discussion (sometimes heated) to resolve and our very different personality styles came into play. Although it was not always comfortable, eventually we had a meeting of the minds which left us both feeling a deep and mutual respect for each other that men get when they experience and resolve that conflict between them. We never broke charity with each other but it was kind of like the boys who beat each other up on the playground and then become best friends afterward.

We parted company, and as he walked away, I watched him leave, admiring the great man that he is and without realizing it, I thought to myself, "I love that guy so much."

The great thing was, as deeply as I knew I loved him at that moment, there was absolutely no erotic attachment for me to work through! I loved him truly as a brother and nothing else. After all those years of struggling to authentically and appropriately love the men in my life through my own distorted sexuality, my relationship with him is God's Word to me that I have finally learned to love a man the way God intended.

The guy I mentioned in the last chapter had told me that my past homosexuality was really gone and would never return. Now, nearly six years after that moment, I could see that it was true.

"Thou Art My Beloved Son"

They say that parenting is the hardest job in the world. I really can't disagree. It is *tough* and, at times, painful, yet I wouldn't trade it for the world. Indeed, one of the most profound experiences happened to me after the birth of my first daughter. I was thirty-one years old and had been teaching at the high school level for about six years at that point.

My daughter was born in June around the time when schools in our area typically recess for the summer. So I took a week off to be home with my wife and new daughter and then returned to work to finish out the last two weeks of school.

As soon as I walked into the building, I could tell that something had changed in me. I wasn't sure what it was, but things were not the way they used to be. At the time, I taught seniors who, generally in the middle of the year, all come down with a mysterious illness.

The illness progresses through the spring and full-blown symptoms are evident by June. The most obvious ones are lethargy, complaints about the difficulties of being in school, chronically "forgetting" to do homework accompanied by a general restlessness and annoyance at the indignity of actually being required to be in school. If you noticed the symptoms of the malady commonly known as *senioritis*, you guessed correctly! Perhaps you have even been a victim of that malady yourself in one of its other forms at various points in your life.

In any case, as I greeted the students I had left only a week before, I found myself becoming suddenly very annoyed with them. I wasn't really sure why I suddenly felt this way; I mean, they couldn't have changed that drastically in a week, right?

What was wrong with me?

One word: *sleep*—or more properly, the lack thereof.

I was tired. I was more tired than I had ever been.

I was stressed.

New babies don't come with instruction manuals, and a woman's pregnancy hormones don't just slip out with the placenta. Just three weeks before, we had also moved from our cozy and updated "starter" house into a larger "fixer-upper" to accommodate our newly growing family. It was truly the worst house on the best street. We bought it purely for its location, schools, proximity to my parents, and size. The house did not offer much else. Portions of the electric did not work, it was dirty, trees were hanging all over it, vegetation was crawling up the sides, and the yard sported a bumper crop of poison ivy.

In addition, we had the unfortunate bad timing of buying one house and trying to sell the other when the housing market was at the end of its prime. The real-estate bubble was about to burst. Although we still got a good deal on the house we bought, unfortunately, the market tanked just under a month later, so I was stuck with taking care of two houses by myself and paying taxes on two properties with my teacher's salary. Although we were fortunate that our first house sold at all, the price declined twenty thousand dollars in what had seemingly overnight become a buyer's market, which left us with very little of the "extra" we had planned on using to renovate the new place.

I simply had nothing left to give. I was spent, and so when I went back to work, where there had previously been patience and understanding of the "young, cool" teacher (relatively speaking, of course) who didn't feel that far removed from his own youth, there was now a cranky new dad who didn't know what the heck he was doing. I just had no energy left for these teens.

I knew at that moment that I had inexorably and permanently left all of the vestiges of the world of childhood behind me forever. I had officially crossed the line into adulthood. I was now on the other side.

I had become one of *them*.

I was a *dad*.

Once you have children, your whole worldview changes. The things you previously cared about so much suddenly become unimportant while those things which at one time seemed so insignificant and far away now loom as daunting monsters to be conquered!

Now you are in charge of a brand new person who depends on you for her very life and you have to do it with a fraction of the sleep you actually need. I remember being so exhausted in those days that I would fall asleep sitting up while I was in the middle of a conversation with someone. One time at work, we had a faculty meeting and the speaker had such a soothing and monotone voice that I fell sound asleep! My boss tapped me from behind and very sympathetically asked if I'd like to excuse myself.

Yeah, no pressure. No stress.

I laugh at all these memories now, but at the time, it was not fun, to say the least. I bring them up because parenthood stretched me and forced me to grow in my own sense of masculinity in areas I had never explored before.

We went on to have a boy and then another girl born less than a year after him. At one point we had three kids under the age of five in the house, only one of whom was toilet trained. Being a dad moved the generational emphasis in my family to where my wife and I were now the primary generation while my parents moved into a supporting role. Suddenly the center of family gravity shifted to us, ready or not!

Kids also have a way of being little mirrors that somehow reflect the worst parts of ourselves back to us. Many a time, I found myself in the position of experiencing the things my parents must have experienced and feeling the way they must have felt. I was determined not to make the same mistakes that my father had made with me, especially with my son.

I am confident through the grace of Jesus Christ that I won't make the *same* mistakes, but I am equally confident that because of my own sinfulness, I have made and will make others.

A priest I know once told a story about a ministry he wanted to begin, which in his diocese had been attempted numerous times in the past. This priest made his desires known to his bishop, who was generally supportive of his ministry but had some concerns.

The bishop asked him, "If I allow you to start this ministry, how will I know that you won't make the same mistakes people in the past have made?"

The priest answered, "Bishop, I promise you that we will not make the same mistakes as the others in the past have made. *We'll make our own mistakes.*"

Our struggle to fully be the presence of God to a hurting world will doubtless be full of mistakes no matter how hard we try, but we have to try anyway and know that the cross of Jesus Christ can undo any mistake and make it work to serve him.

In so trying, one of the ways my wife and I have always attempted to do this has been to affirm our children not only as people but also in their respective masculinity and femininity. It is not enough for children to know simply that they are valued. I always knew that. They also need to know that they are valued as the boy or girl God created them to be. Now, I am not talking about a slavish conformity to the gender roles of this or that culture but a true valuing of their masculine or feminine essence, however they might express it.

For example, like me, my son was not into sports as many of the boys his age were. I could see how, like me, his lack of interest and, in some cases, ability did have a negative effect on his ability to engage in male culture.

He really excels in creative expression, especially music. That's OK. Wherever he excels and wherever he wants to be is where my wife and I will be his number one fans! The same is true with our daughters.

A couple of years ago, he took an interest in basketball. Now although I had played as a child, I had not really kept up with it over the years and had forgotten most of the rules. One day, his coach asked me to make sure that my son understood how to play in the arc.

The *what*?

I nodded my head in agreement and told the coach I'd be sure to do just that. Coach could count on me!

What the heck was the arc? How was I going to figure this out?

I decided I was going to use this as an opportunity to grow as a man and help myself at the same time, so the next day, I marched myself down to the men's physical education faculty room. I knew and liked a number of the teachers from working with them together on various school-wide initiatives in the past.

A bunch of them were sitting around a large table doing grading and other paperwork as I walked in.

"Hey guys!" I said, swallowing my own insecurities as I contemplated telling this very masculine group of guys that, at least in this area of the masculine world, I was just not as up-to-snuff as they were and could they possibly help me out?

"So . . ." I started. "My son is playing basketball and the coach wants me to review how to play the game with him, and other than the basics about getting the basketball away from the other team and into your own team's basket, I know just about nothing."

I waited for at least some good-natured ribbing from the group, but none came.

They just looked up at me for a second and then one of them pulled a chair back and gestured for me to sit while another guy grabbed a book off the shelf and threw it open on the table in front of us and he self-deprecatingly joked, "See, gym teachers use books too!" to a round of raucous laughter.

One of them pushed a book toward me that was opened to a diagram of a basketball court.

"What does the coach want you to teach him?" he asked me.

"How to the play the arch," I said, unsure of the term.

"The *arc*?" he clarified, with not the least bit of condescension in his voice. I had forgotten the stupid name of it. *Duh!*

"Um . . . yeah. . . . That's it . . . sorry," I stammered. "I told you I didn't know much."

"No problem," he said and went on to explain the rules involved.

I probably repeated it back to him nine ways from Sunday until I was sure I had it right. After I was satisfied, I thanked him for his time. He told me to come back anytime.

Now, I probably could have gotten the same information off the internet, but I chose to go see these guys in order to help myself grow in the areas of the masculine world in which I am still not comfortable. In many ways, trying to take care of my own son's needs is still helping me to heal and grow as a man.

In this case, I felt like I was almost reliving those high school years wherein I rejected what the coaches had to say simply because they reminded me of my dad. I realized again that all men, including me, have their own strengths and weaknesses and how wrong it is to reject an area of masculinity outright simply because I might be uncomfortable.

My son found that basketball was not for him and moved on to soccer, which he loves and in which he demonstrates some ability. In God's Providence, which often lands us in situations in which we would never think we would find ourselves, guess who the assistant coach was (twice)?

So, in closing, no matter where my children's talents and interests may lie, I don't want them to ever lose sight of the gift of their own respective masculinity or femininity. I want them to always know that they have my fatherly blessing and affirmation. Whenever I am in a position to do so, I say it so there will be no doubt. Often, I will use a Scripture to do it.

In particular, at my son's First Holy Communion, when the time came to give the toast, I praised God and thanked him for the gift of my son, and then I looked right into his eyes and said the words of Mark 1:11, "Thou art my beloved Son; with thee I am well pleased."

The look on his face told me that he knew it was true.

"Even the Hairs of Your Head Are All Numbered"

As my development and healing continued, after I had children and had established myself as a husband and father, I was in the habit of cutting my own hair with an electric shaver. I never cut it all the way down, instead opting to use the plastic guide coverings over the shears that allow you to cut your hair down to the desired length.

One day, I accidentally forgot to put the guide on and put the shaver to my head. To my horror, I saw a perfect shaved rectangle right in the middle of my head. After calling my wife in to see if there was any way we could think of to fix it, we decided that the best thing for me to do was to shave my entire head.

I didn't like it.

I always thought that baldness either meant getting old or looking really harsh. Nonetheless, I was stuck with the look, at least for the few weeks it would take for my hair to grow back to near its normal length.

Then, a very strange thing began to happen.

I began to feel the Lord calling me in prayer to leave my head shaven. This was a little odd to me that the Lord of heaven should be interested in my hair style. I mean, really, didn't he have bigger things like poverty and war that he should be concerned about?

Well, throughout all my years, one thing I have learned over and over again is not to tell God how to do his job or second-guess his wisdom. The other thing I have learned is that the Lord cares deeply about all of us as individuals and knows all of the intimate details of our lives, even those parts of ourselves we would rather hide under the proverbial fig leaves. "Are not five sparrows sold for two pennies? And not one of them is forgotten before God. Why, even the hairs of your head are all numbered. Fear not; you are of more value than many sparrows" (Lk 12:6–7).

So I followed what I thought were his promptings and continued to shave my head each day. Of course, the first one to notice this was my wife. When she asked me why, I really didn't have a good answer. I simply told her that the Lord had called me to it and that it was part of my healing as a man. Prayerful woman that she is, she accepted that. She didn't like it but she accepted it.

As time went on, I began to change. I started behaving differently and even thinking differently. I used to think of myself as a sensitive and unintimidating guy. Now, I found myself not caring whether people thought that or not. I used to worry a lot about how people felt or if I had hurt their feelings or damaged our relationship by something I had said or done. That, too, went by the proverbial wayside. I wouldn't say I was mean or uncharitable, I was just not as sensitive.

And I *liked* it.

Others around me began to notice, too, particularly women. I was told many times and very nicely by female relatives, friends, and coworkers that they preferred me with hair. I had no intention of making any change until the Lord told me to. One time, my wife asked me how long I thought I would keep shaving and I told her that I truly did not know but that the Lord would tell me in his good time. Interestingly, all the men told me how much they liked it, and some would even affectionately rub my head.

People also began to notice the changes in my personality. I definitely was not as approachable as I used to be, and people began to find me a little intimidating. I remember one particular time that I was talking with one of my coworkers who asked me to complete a particular task at work.

When I agreed to it, she accidentally let it slip that other coworkers had talked about asking me but she was the only one willing to approach me. I didn't get it. These people had known me for *years*! When I pressed her to find out what she meant and who had said it, she wouldn't reveal her sources. Far from being upset about this, I actually enjoyed it.

I realized that because I was raised in a very female-dominated family and then chose a female-dominated profession, I had really nurtured that sensitive side of myself at the expense of my masculine side. Shaving my head helped me get back in touch with that lost part of myself. I needed to assert my own manhood, not in a boorish or dominating way, but in a way that had very clear boundaries around my masculine self.

This continued on until Lent one year. I saw a man I really liked. I found him *attractive* and masculine. His face had a hard edge to it that I found alluring. It wasn't unkind, and he wasn't what most would consider extremely handsome, but he had very clear eyes and the determined look of a man who knew who he was and was completely comfortable with himself.

He was the kind of man I *wanted* to be.

It took me a few seconds to realize that I was looking at myself! I looked in the mirror and saw my face, and for the first time, after thirty-some years, I finally saw myself as God (and many others) had seen me all along.

I *was* the man I wanted to be.

More importantly, I was the man God made me to be, not the one I *thought* he should have made me to be.

I knew at that moment that I no longer needed the shaven head. The process had accomplished its goal. Even if my hair grew back, the Lord had brought to the forefront my masculine essence and I experienced it and made it my own. The shaved head was my own personal "coming out" to the world as a man, whether people liked it or not. Since I had done that, my outer appearance no longer mattered.

Once my hair began to grow back, I discussed the whole experience with my wife to get her insights on the whole thing. We have a terrific marriage, thanks to the grace of God, and one of the really great things that we do for each other is to analyze and discuss how we have changed and healed spiritually.

She affirmed my observations and said that she knew that what I was doing was from the Lord and that it would end when it had accomplished its purpose. She said that she thought it was like a pendulum and that the shaved head was kind of an "extreme" and bold expression of my masculinity, probably similar to what most boys do during their adolescence or college years in order to individuate from parents and the expectations of society, in favor of the "true" man inside. She predicted that over time I wouldn't be quite as "edgy" and that the pendulum might swing back closer to what it was before, but with this new insight, I would never lose what I had gained.

She was right. Up until that point, I had always felt like I was more or less playing a role when it came to my own masculine identity. I was adopting many of the trappings of masculinity and enjoying doing it, but I often felt like a little boy trying on his father's clothes. They felt right and good but never quite fit right. Now, I felt the true freedom of knowing that masculinity is my own and I will never lose it again.

I have my own set of clothes.

They fit me well and they look great on me.

They are mine.

I am his.

When the Son makes you free, you are free indeed.

The Feast of Our Lady of Fatima, May 13, 2019

Healing Homosexuality

Given all the controversy regarding changing one's sexual orientation today, a question I often get is, "How did it happen?"

It was a really simple plan, but most of it didn't depend on me. A lot of it was simply being open to others and to the promptings of the Holy Spirit as well as application of some psychological and spiritual principles.

Can anyone do it?

Absolutely.

Will it have the same effect for everyone that it had for me?

Probably not.

There are no guarantees.

Some may not experience the depth of healing that I did; others may experience more. The way same-sex attraction develops in each man is different. Again, I like the analogy of *homosexualities* rather than the singular.

This is the plan that worked for me though, and I think it is one that would at least partially work for many men who struggled as I have.

1. If you have never done so before, ask for and accept

at this moment the true Lordship of Jesus Christ into your life. Accept him as your personal Savior and ask him to reveal himself to you and take complete control of your life. Surrender everything to him. Fall in love with him.

2. Attend Mass and receive the Holy Eucharist as often as possible. If you are not Catholic, seek out whatever worship opportunities are available in your community and go be a part of them as often as you can, particularly if they are geared toward men.

3. Frequent the sacrament of Reconciliation (confession) often, even when you are not conscious of mortal sin. Most spiritual giants recommend at least once a month. St. John Paul II went at least *every week*; some say *he went every day*. If you are not Catholic, confess or discuss your sins with an understanding pastor, minister, or accountability partner. If you ask them, many Catholic priests are willing to listen, help, and pray with you and for you even though they cannot grant sacramental absolution to non-Catholics.

4. Fast, do penance, or perform some other kind of mortification regularly. People often object to this because they say that God doesn't need our suffering. Perfectly true. He doesn't. However, we live in a fallen world and it is precisely through suffering that we find our way back to him. Fasting or other mortification is really for us, not for him. When we engage in regular self-denial, it serves the dual purpose of strengthening our own resolve in our

own struggles and also kind of puts our proverbial money where our mouths are. Thus, it makes our prayers more efficacious. It also improves our self-mastery which leads to greater spiritual strength. We thus give the Lord a sign of our resolve to do what we say we will do, and he honors that. This can be something as simple as taking cold showers, skipping a meal (or two or three), abstaining from social media for a time, or just about anything else that causes you to deny your own will. I have found that simply staying within my allotted calories for the week is quite penitential!

5. Make sure you have a deep prayer life, with silent meditation while sitting in front of the Blessed Sacrament whenever possible. This can be done daily, a couple of times a week, during a weekly holy hour, or whatever works for you. Talk to Jesus about everything that matters to you. This is how you give him your life and your heart. Know that he is waiting there for you and wants to hear from you.

6. Read the Gospels and study and meditate on the life of Jesus Christ. Note how he treated others, what he said, what he did, who he is. He is the perfect Man. Try to model all of your being after his life.

7. Cultivate a relationship with and true devotion to the Blessed Mother of Jesus Christ, especially through meditation on the Rosary. Ask her to always protect you, defend you, and keep you on a sure path to her Divine Son. Remember that no saint knows Jesus Christ better than his own specifically

chosen mother. She is the one woman God selected from across time and space to be the mother of the Messiah. He could have had anyone. He chose her. Should we do any less? As mentioned before, the best form of devotion would be to consecrate yourself to Jesus Christ through her in the method of St. Louis de Montfort outlined in *True Devotion to Mary*. The scope and limitations of this book do not permit for a thorough explanation of the truly amazing fruit this has borne in my life, but I cannot recommend highly it enough. Besides the sacraments, this is the best spiritual thing you can do for yourself.

8. Thank God every day for the gift of your masculine sexuality and ask him to untwist any distortions within it.

9. Read St. John Paul II's *Theology of the Body*. A word of warning, though, it is a dense philosophical and theological work and you might benefit from also reading one of the many companion books written to explain it. I particularly like the work of Christopher West but any solid Catholic author or speaker will do the trick. Some people find John Paul's work so intense that the explanatory books might be more helpful than the work itself.

10. Read the biographies of male saints, particularly the modern ones. They are amazing and accessible models of manhood. I, of course, especially recommend those about John Paul the Great, particularly George Weigel's exhaustive two-volume set *Witness to Hope* and *The End and the Beginning: Pope John Paul II —*

The Victory of Freedom, the Last Years, the Legacy. For a lighter and more devotional read which is no less satisfying, check out Jason Evert's *Saint John Paul the Great: His Five Loves*. Other great manly saints include Maximillian Kolbe, Emil Kapaun, Louis de Montfort, Don Bosco, or any other male saint with whom you feel a connection.

11. Read books written on the healing of homosexuality. The classic work on the subject still remains Joseph Nicolosi's *Reparative Therapy of the Male Homosexual* as well as *Shame and Attachment Loss: The Practical Work of Reparative Therapy*. There are other good books out there as well, including Gerard van den Aardweg's *The Battle for Normality*. This has a particularly good journaling section which I highly recommend. There are others out there as well.

12. This is an important one. Consciously work on friendships and relationships with men, if possible, with your father and male family members and with your peer group. *I cannot emphasize enough how important this is.* For me, it is kind of like learning a foreign language. You won't really be able to speak it unless you *immerse* yourself in it completely. It is especially helpful to join healthy mens' groups. For me, this was primarily accomplished through my household brothers, but now there are lots of good groups out there. Try to find one near you.

13. Get in touch with your physical maleness. Men experience the world through their bodies in a very unique way. Get into some kind of healthy

exercise regimen that you like, whether it be natural bodybuilding, running/jogging, swimming, sports teams, or some other activity. It is an added benefit if you can do this with other men. Pay attention to your body while you do these things and savor the feeling of being a man.

14. Consider all the areas where you feel "outside" of the male world in your life, whether it be gardening, cars, hunting, sports, hobbies, et cetera. If you don't have any interests in these areas, at least try to get a basic idea about these things so you can make some healthy connections with other men. Or find a typical masculine area of interest that interests you and go do it!

15. When you experience same-sex attractions, take that into prayer and ask the Lord to show you why you feel attracted to this particular man. What is it you like about him? Is there a particular part of his body you find alluring? Are you attracted to a certain "type"? Is what you like about him an area where you feel deficient? You will need to do this constantly so that it becomes a part of your way of thinking and being. You will have to retrain your mind.

16. Ask the Lord to illuminate those areas in your life where you don't feel "man enough." Then ask him to heal those parts of your heart and to fill you with a masculine spirit. This is not a one-time thing. Again, you will also need to do this constantly so that it becomes a part of your way of thinking and being. Remember, you will have to retrain your mind.

17. If there is an area of your life where your father or some other man/boy caused you pain, during prayer or counseling, ask the Lord to enter that pain with you and to help you move past it toward healing. If you think you need help to do this (and you probably do; it's not a task for the faint of heart), see a priest, deacon, or other trusted minister or even a counselor or therapist (just be sure the therapist is a trusted one with a solid grounding in Christian sexuality who will not try to use gay-affirmative therapy on you). Once again, you may need to repeat this a number of times.

18. If possible, seek psychotherapy, particularly reparative therapy, if it is available. Again, make sure the therapist is respectful of your beliefs even if he or she may not necessarily be familiar with orientation change.

If you read this and a lot of it sounds familiar, it should; at least the first seven steps should. They are the basic steps of any Christian who is seeking a deeper relationship with Jesus Christ, particularly if they seek healing of some aspect of their lives. The remainder are a summary of what I have found in my own personal struggle with SSA. It worked for me.

Now, I do want to point out that what I'm talking about here is not some magical formula to "pray the gay away." As many ministries who went down that route and later collapsed under the weight of false claims have shown, *that just doesn't work.*

What I am talking about here is what the Gospels render in Greek as *metanoia*, roughly translated as "true, deep conversion." It means a complete reordering of one's life to conform it to that of Jesus Christ. It's not about changing anything but rather healing and becoming a better man and a better Christian. Change may or may not happen to a greater or lesser degree but one of the beautiful things about struggling with SSA is that the path of our sanctity is clear and specific. Once we set down the road, we simply enter more deeply into the life and passion of Jesus Christ.

So although the amount of "change" may vary from person to person, the Lord wants us to ask for what we desire and then let him do the rest. Practically speaking, it is similar to what St. Thomas à Kempis proposed in his *Imitation of Christ*.

> There was once a man who was very anxious, and wavered between fear and hope. One day, overcome with sadness, he lay prostrate in prayer before the altar in church, and pondering these matters in his mind, said, "Oh, if only I knew that I should always persevere!" then he heard within his heart an answer from God: "If you knew this, what would you do? Do now what you would then, and all will be well." . . .
>
> There is one thing that deters many in their spiritual progress and zeal for amendment, namely, fear of the difficulties and the cost of victory. *But rest assured that those who grow in virtue beyond their fellows are they who fight most manfully to overcome whatever is most difficult and distasteful to them.* . . .

> All men do not have the same things to overcome and mortify. . . . Two things in particular are a great help to amendment of life—a forcible withdrawal from any vice to which our nature inclines, and a fervent pursuit of any grace of which we stand in particular need.[33]

Thus, the struggle with homosexuality is not a sidebar issue to distract us from the way to holiness. If it is the cross which God has allowed us to bear, then, for us, it *is* the way to holiness. So, using this point of view, I adopted the above-mentioned steps and based it on that same principle. If you seek the healing of your masculine soul, do the above steps and *act* as if you've already received that healing, confident in the Lord's grace. Over the years, it has worked for me, and I can truly say I am a satisfied heterosexual man, not without his insecurities and flaws and not completely without SSA, but a full and real man, nonetheless, after the image of Jesus Christ.

So, now you might be thinking, "What if I try this and it doesn't work?"

If you truly try it, I would say it almost *has* to work. Now, you may not experience the depth of the healing that I did or you may experience even more than I did. I don't really know. You may not necessarily eliminate or even reduce SSA, but one thing I can guarantee is that you will enter into a deeper relationship with Jesus Christ and you will find

---

[33] Thomas a Kempis and Leo Sherley-Price, *The Imitation of Christ* (Penguin Books, 2005), Book I, chapter 25, emphasis mine.

healing and redemption for your suffering. Isn't that what Christianity is really about?

So, if you are struggling with SSA or maybe have even adopted a gay lifestyle or identity, I would like to challenge you to try this for one year.

I challenge you to take the chance.

It's only a year, right? After the year is over, then you can revisit your life choices and make a new choice based on this new year of information. What do you have to lose? In his inaugural homily on April 24, 2005, Pope Benedict XVI summed it up best by echoing the words of his venerable predecessor when he said to the congregation and the world, "And so, today, with great strength and great conviction, on the basis of long personal experience of life, I say to you, dear young people: Do not be afraid of Christ! He takes nothing away, and he gives you everything. When we give ourselves to him, we receive a hundredfold in return. Yes, open, open wide the doors to Christ—and you will find true life. Amen."[34]

So, go on! Be a man! Open those doors and let that grace flow in!

---

[34] Benedict XVI, "Homily of His Holiness Benedict XVI," Mass, Imposition of the Pallium and Conferral of the Fisherman's Ring for the Beginning of the Petrine Ministry of the Bishop of Rome, April 24, 2005, Papal Archive, The Holy See, http://w2.vatican.va/content/benedict-xvi/en/homilies/2005/documents/hf_ben-xvi_hom_20050424_inizio-pontificato.html. [Accessed May 1, 2019].

Bibliography

Aggarwal, Sanjay and Rene Gerrets. "Exploring a Dutch paradox: an ethnographic investigation of gay men's mental health". *Culture, Health & Sexuality: An International Journal for Research, intervention & Care*, no. 16:2 (2014): 105-109. https://www.tandfonline.com/doi/abs/10.1080/13691058.2013.841290?journalCode=tchs20. [Accessed April 30, 2019]

American Psychological Association. "What causes a person to have a particular sexual orientation?" Answers to your questions: For a better understanding of sexual orientation and homosexuality. Last modified 2008. https://www.apa.org/topics/lgbt/orientation. [Accessed April 29, 2019]

Anderson, Carl and Eduardo Chavez. *Our Lady of Guadalupe: Mother of the Civilization of Love.* New York, NY: Doubleday, 2009.

Augustine, and R. S. Pine-Coffin. *Confessions: Saint Augustine.* Penguin Classics, an Imprint of Penguin Books, 2015.

Benedict XVI. *God is Love: Deus Carits Est.* December 25, 2005. Papal Archive. The Holy See. http://w2.vatican.va/content/benedict-xvi/en/encyclicals/documents/hf_ben-xvi_enc_20051225_deus-caritas-est.html. [Accessed April 30, 2019]

Benedict XVI. "Homily of His Holiness Benedict XVI."
Mass, Imposition of the Pallium and Conferral of
the Fisherman's Ring for the Beginning of the Petrine
Ministry of the Bishop of Rome. April 24, 2005. Papal
Archive. The Holy See. http://w2.vatican.va/content/
benedict-xvi/en/homilies/2005/documents/hf_ben-
xvi_hom_20050424_inizio-pontificato.html. [Accessed
May 1, 2019]

Catechism of the Catholic Church, 2nd ed. Washington, DC:
United States Catholic Conference, 2000.

Chaput, Charles J. "Strangers in a Strange Land." First
Things. January 01, 2015. https://www.firstthings.com/
article/2015/01/strangers-in-a-strange-land. [Accessed
April 29, 2019]

Evert, Jason. Saint John Paul the Great: His Five Loves.
Lakewood, CO: Totus Tuus Press, 2014.

John Paul II. "Homily of His Holiness John Paul II for the
Inauguration of His Pontificate." Mass at the Beginning
of the Pontificate. October 22, 1978. Papal Archive. The
Holy See. http://w2.vatican.va/content/john-paul-ii/en/
homilies/1978/documents/hf_jp-ii_hom_19781022_
inizio-pontificato.html. [Accessed April 11, 2019]

John Paul II. Man and Woman He Created Them: A Theology of the Body. Boston, MA: Pauline Books and Media,
2006.

Louis De Montfort. True Devotion to Mary: With Preparation for Total Consecration. Charlotte, NC: TAN Books,
2010.

Mayer, Lawrence S. and Paul R. McHugh. "Sexuality and
Gender: Findings from the Biological, Psychological

and Social Sciences". *The New Atlantis: A Journal of Technology & Society*, no. 50 (Fall 2016): 4–144. https://www.thenewatlantis.com/docLib/20160819_TNA50SexualityandGender.pdf. [Accessed April 29, 2019]

Nicolosi, Joseph. *Reparative Therapy of Male Homosexuality: A New Clinical Approach*. Lanham, MD: Rowman & Littlefield Publishers, 2004.

Nicolosi, Joseph. *Shame and Attachment Loss: The Practical Work of Reparative Therapy*. Liberal Mind Publishers, 2016.

Paul VI. *Dogmatic Constitution on the Church: Lumen Gentium.* November 21, 1964. Papal Archive. The Holy See. http://www.vatican.va/archive/hist_councils/ii_vatican_council/documents/vat-ii_cons_19651207_gaudium-et-spes_en.html. [Accessed May 1, 2019]

Paul VI. *Pastoral Constitution on the Church in the Modern World: Gaudium et Spes.* December 7, 1965. Papal Archive. The Holy See. http://www.vatican.va/archive/hist_councils/ii_vatican_council/documents/vat-ii_const_19641121_lumen-gentium_en.html [Accessed April 29, 2019]

Ratzinger, Joseph. *The Blessing of Christmas.* San Francisco, CA: Ignatius Press, 2007.

Ratzinger, Joseph. *Letter to the Bishops of the Church on the Pastoral Care of Homosexual Persons.* October 1, 1986. Congregation of the Doctrine of the Faith: Complete List of Documents. http://www.vatican.va/roman_curia/congregations/cfaith/documents/

rc_con_cfaith_doc_19861001_homosexual-persons_
en.html [Accessed May 1, 2019]

Thomas a Kempis and Leo Sherley-Price. *The Imitation of Christ*. Penguin Books, 2005.

Van den Aardweg, Gerard J. M. *The Battle for Normality: A Guide for (Self-) Therapy for Homosexuality*. San Francisco, CA: Ignatius Press, 1997.

Weigel, George. *The End and the Beginning: Pope John Paul II – The Victory of Freedom, the Last Years, the Legacy*. New York, NY: Doubleday, 2010.

Weigel, George. *Witness to Hope: The Biography of John Paul II*. New York, NY: HarperCollins Publishers, 1999.

World Apostolate of Fatima, USA. "The Story of Fatima". About Fatima. https://www.bluearmy.com/the-story-of-fatima. [Accessed April 30, 2019]

Zuchniewicz. Pawel. *Miracles of John Paul II: Santo Subito*. Toronto, Ontario: Catholic Youth Studio – KSM Inc., 2006